PENGUIN BUSINESS

TECHPROOF ME

A. Siddharth Pai is a co-founder of Siana Capital and a venture capital fund manager for deep-science and deep-technology start-ups that ideally have social impact. He has led some of the most innovative technology-sourcing transactions and has advised and completed over US$20 billion in transaction value. Siddharth has over three decades of experience working in the US and Europe and moved to Asia/India in 2002. He has held senior executive roles with IBM and KPMG Consulting/Bearing Point in the Americas, Asia–Pacific and Europe, and was partner and president of TPI/ISG's Asia–Pacific region. He holds an MBA in finance and an MS in applied economics from the University of Rochester as well as a BCom from Bangalore University.

ADVANCE PRAISE FOR THE BOOK

'With more than thirty years of expertise and keen industry observation, Siddharth Pai brings a well-explained survival guide to those aspiring to succeed in tech today and in the future. With its simple conversational tone, *Techproof Me* has achieved the trifecta of a successful book in its genre: easy reading, relevant substance and experienced vision. *Techproof Me* is bound to answer your questions, resolve your quandaries and open doors to a universe that seemed closed off earlier. Here begins your journey to tech success without being a "techie"'—Girish Krishnamurthy, CEO and MD, Tata Medical and Diagnostics Ltd

'I have known Sid for over fifteen years and, for many of those years, he served on my board as chief strategy officer, in addition to leading our business in Asia–Pacific. He is a visionary who has an astounding ability to explain esoteric and deeply technological issues in clear and easily understandable terms. If you want to stay ahead of today's mind-boggling changes in technology, this book is a must-read!'—Michael P. Connors, chairman and CEO, Information Services Group (ISG), Inc.

'I have known Sid for many years, both as a technology consultant whose services we used as well as an investor in deep tech. This book is an insightful and engaging read for those who want to keep abreast of the warp speed change in technology in our times'—Ranjan Pai, chairman, Manipal Education and Medical Group (MEMG)

'Siddharth Pai has built an exceptional career in consulting and technology for over three decades. He has had a ringside view of how companies around the world have adopted technology. He has witnessed, first-hand, how our skills of using, making and selling technology have evolved over the last thirty-plus years. I can think of no one better to help us understand how we can scale as individuals in a world increasingly powered by technology. We don't need to learn to code to be technology experts. All we need is a broad understanding of the power of technology and fine appreciation of business models to be successful in the coming decade'—Vaishali Kasture, head, enterprise segment, Amazon Internet Services Pvt. Ltd, India and South Asia

'An essential read for all non-techies seeking to thrive in the digital business era. I have muddled through nearly four decades in the IT industry by learning the hard way how to become a "TechImpostor". Would that the wisdom and ideas contained in this book had been available to me at the start of my career'—Duncan Aitchison, research director, TechMarketView, former executive vice president, Capgemini, and former president, Europe, Middle East and Africa, Information Services Group (ISG), Inc.

'The disruption caused by the rapid spread of digital technologies is unsettling to most people. In this book, Siddharth Pai explains how we can master the use of technology in life and business to enable us to succeed in the era of digital disruption'—T.V. Mohandas Pai, chairman, Aarin Capital Partners

'*Techproof Me* is essential reading for any business executive aspiring to effectively leverage digital technologies to improve competitiveness. A valuable and practical exploration of how non-technical leaders can not only navigate the rapid changes in digital capabilities but actually drive decisions and investments to support their broader business strategy, all without having to become an expert technologist'—Paul Schmidt, partner, Kyndryl Inc.

'*Techproof Me* is a compelling, straightforward analysis of the trends shaping technology today. It is comprehensive, stays away from jargon and provides a clear understanding of complex concepts. The personal insights make for a very worthwhile read with strategies that are easy to adopt'—Kalpana Raina, board director, Impact Investor

TECHPROOF ME

The Art of Mastering EVER-CHANGING TECHNOLOGY

A. SIDDHARTH PAI

BUSINESS
An imprint of Penguin Random House

PENGUIN BUSINESS

USA | Canada | UK | Ireland | Australia
New Zealand | India | South Africa | China

Penguin Business is part of the Penguin Random House group of companies whose addresses can be found at global.penguinrandomhouse.com

Published by Penguin Random House India Pvt. Ltd
4th Floor, Capital Tower 1, MG Road,
Gurugram 122 002, Haryana, India

First published in Penguin Business by Penguin Random House India 2022

10 9 8 7 6 5 4 3 2 1

ISBN 9780143452010

Typeset in Adobe Garamond Pro by MAP Systems, Bengaluru, India
Printed at Replika Press Pvt. Ltd, India

www.penguin.co.in

To Sringeri Sharadamba

Contents

Section I

Section II

Section I

Chapter 1

Prologue—Life Is but an Act . . .

I presume you picked up this book to understand how you can co-exist with technology, especially given that its recent changes seem to be unsettling individuals, companies and entire nations. So, I'll get down to the basic premise of this book right away. It is based on three cardinal concepts:

A. You don't need to become a computer programmer to stay ahead of technological changes.
B. An understanding of business functions and a simple framework to analyse and understand how the business process works is a crucial tool in staying techproof.
C. There are only four roles that all of us play in our businesses or organizations. Being sufficiently informed on how technology is morphing will allow you to play those roles well.

Our behaviour changes based on the context in which we find ourselves. When we are alone, or think that we are, we tend to let our guard down and do as we please. This behaviour is often seen online, where people can say hateful things behind the supposed privacy offered to them by a screen and an assumed online avatar. Hence the dangers that lurk in chat rooms and in all sorts of social media.

The illusion we have of not being in the public eye is most certainly also seen in our day-to-day physical lives. For instance, who hasn't seen a driver in the next lane over, doing something which he would never do in public, while waiting for the light to change? This happens because he has the illusion of privacy in the cocoon of his car. We behave differently when we think people aren't looking. We change when we think they are.

Our behaviour changes when we are in a group. In a work situation, we behave formally, bending ourselves to suit the culture our work group embodies. So, the suits come out—or the sandals—depending on the group's culture. Our language and use of slang changes to emulate that of the group. No one would be caught dead in a suit and shining oxfords or pumps where jeans and sandals are the norm.

In a non-work situation, such as with family, we follow the codes set by our families and the roles that we hold within them. We have yet another set of rules when interacting with people in social situations, from complete informality on a night out with the 'boys' or the 'girls' to set social rules when at a colleague's house for dinner.

And then there are the meta-group rules. The ones where we're expected to cheer every move by a candidate or in-office politician from our political parties. Or to express undying patriotism for our countries, even when we might not agree deep down with all that our candidate or country is doing.

Yet, through all these roles, we are essentially still ourselves. All we are doing is putting on masks to suit the character or role we are playing in a particular situation. For most of us, these roles are well practised and come naturally since they are imposed on us since childhood. For instance, I can pivot from being a father to being a husband without skipping a beat. But navigating these role changes in a work or organizational context does not come as easy. Despite all that human resource managers may say, the 'roles and responsibilities' document is a myth. These documents are just expressing what you are responsible for delivering. You will have to play many different roles in order to deliver successfully on what you are expected to do.

Those who have mastered the ability to play these roles well, and to suddenly pivot and switch from one role to the next, usually turn out to be successful in carrying out their responsibilities. This is by no means accidental or attributable to 'luck'. Economists and psychologists have spent a long time studying organizational behaviour, and while they come at it from very different viewpoints, their observations on organizational and individual dynamics are on point.

In 2002, psychologist Daniel Kahneman and economist Vernon L. Smith were awarded the Nobel Prize in Economics. Kahneman was awarded the prize 'for having integrated insights from psychological research into economic science, especially concerning human judgment and decision-making under uncertainty', while Smith was awarded the prize 'for having established laboratory experiments as a tool in empirical economic analysis, especially in the study of alternative market mechanisms'. More Nobel prizes followed for behavioural economists who studied the role of psychology in decision-making in finance as well as for establishing that otherwise 'rational' human beings could and did behave irrationally in defiance of what classical economic theory would normally have predicted they do.

Nobel laureate Daniel Kahneman has written a very readable book on the subject, called *Thinking, Fast and Slow*. *Nudge* by Cass Sunstein and Richard Thaler (another Nobel laureate) is a particularly good read, especially if you want to understand how modern technology can push consumers into certain behaviour patterns.

This book, however, is about the types of new roles we need to play in our fast-changing technology-oriented world so that we are truly techproof. It will provide you with information and observations on a variety of technology-oriented subjects so that you are able to pivot on a space as small as a coin when you need to.

This book is not a self-help book. This book is for people who are about to embark on or have already made significant headway in their careers. As such, you, dear reader, are more than capable of doing the self-analysis you need in order to decide where you fit as a person, and to decide which roles you want to learn to play in your organization. That said, this book is also, at least in small part, about the introspection we need to do to mould our basic personas and make them pliable into new roles the world will demand from us. While I might provide a few pointers in general on how to 'act' a part, or indeed how to better understand yourself, my real intent is to give you a framework for thinking while you are actually playing your part in your current or future organization or business. It is this 'framework for thinking' that will enable you to make your career techproof.

I will describe some of the recent advances in technology, and how the various technological piece-parts come together to provide value to you as an individual, other individuals you may be working with as well as the business you may be serving or building. The aim of this book is to help you understand how you can fit in the jigsaw, for which several chapters will dwell on information and thoughts about today's advances in technology.

Chapter 2

Putting on the Show

Technology is going to keep advancing along several lines, but this needn't frighten us in the least. People who are technologists keep throwing out acronyms and terms that supposedly make them part of an inner circle, but in truth, most technological ideas are based on very simple concepts of how a particular business process is supposed to function when it is automated. For example, if you wanted to automate your collections process—which today requires clerks to send out invoices, follow up with customers, handle banking transactions and so on—which of these piece-parts of the collections process can be automated? Could you have your computer system generate the bills instead? Could your follow-up letters to your customers be computer-generated once their payables have reached, say, a thirty-day period within which they haven't paid your invoice? Interestingly, other (general) advances in technology can help you on the path. In this collections example, for instance, India's various payment platforms like RTGS and NEFT, along with any number of UPI applications, have removed the need for your clerks to go to the local bank branch to deposit your customers' cheques. They have automated that function.

Even if you are not a technologist by training, once you understand the functionality of a system, and the specific type of logic it uses in order to perform that function, you are better off than 99 per cent of the laity. And this means you are now in the 1 per cent that can be well versed in what that particular technology actually does and can be counted among the 'gurus'. But there is one more 'magic' ingredient in getting to be noticed as a guru, and that is if you can get the other parts of being a guru right, which is to simply play one or more of the roles described in this book. There is no rocket science here—all you need is to know how to act or play a role.

I assume you already know how to put on a show. That said, a small primer might help! While many people think that being an actor requires you to get into the 'skin' of the character you are playing, this is a useless cliché. In my experience, three specific strengths are the keystones to putting on a convincing show.

The first is to *know yourself sufficiently*. This acts as a basis from which you need to deviate from time to time, solely in order to act your part. The second is to *know your audience*, which means knowing how your audience expects to be communicated with. The third is to be able to *express yourself correctly and cogently* in a manner that the audience understands, which requires sufficient knowledge of and facility with the things that excite or frighten the audience.

Our conversation during this book will move through several topics, but each of these topics are cardinal ideas to help you play the part or parts you have chosen, or which are needed in the context of your work. These ideas will draw on a variety of academic disciplines, as well as advances in technology and personal experiences. Technology will keep changing but playing your role when armed with this sort of thought construct, as well as specific information about the landscape of new and emerging technology, will make you techproof.

So here are the roles you need to play in order to make the most of technological change within your business or within the organization you work for. There is no detailed instruction on how to play these roles; I am simply providing a short definition of each role. Figure out which ones you need to play well in order to be successful at work. All I can say with certainty is that over your career, you will find yourself playing all these roles—sometimes daily.

There are four roles: Soldier, Originator, Leader and Empath. Or **SOLE**, if you would like a mnemonic to remember these roles easily.

The Soldier: as Hurdler/Collaborator/ Threat Detector

A good soldier understands the inner workings of his or her organization. This applies to how an organization is set up and understanding the role of each cog in the machine. Soldiers must be hurdlers who find ways to improve the efficiency of a system and a better means to reach the end result. Hurdlers intuitively understand that being part of a system means working for the good of the system and not for themselves as individuals. For this, they need a micro-level understanding of how an organization functions and what can be done to improve the working of the organization. In truth, all organizations have common goals. This is what a hurdler intuitively understands, and he or she works to improve those goals.

Therefore, when something changes in the industry and/or organization, a hurdler knows what to do and how to adapt. Hurdlers can analyse what is required to reach the goal in the new (and changed) scenario and therefore can make the changes to achieve it. The ability to collaborate is critical for hurdlers as this allows them to ensure the smooth functioning of an organization/system. One needs to understand the specifics of a particular role in a business and know how to improve its value and efficiency to achieve the common goal. Collaboration requires an intimate understanding of the inner workings of a system and how to properly use the system.

Collaborators also understand how various roles and jobs work with each other and how they can help improve the system.

Soldiers are also threat detectors—in that they understand the position of an organization within an industry in the same way that hurdlers understand the value of each role in an organization. They get what the market needs a particular organization fulfils and therefore what its weaknesses are in terms of business and value in general. Threat detectors have a macro-level perspective on the system and can pinpoint places where an organization may be threatened/disrupted and find ways to solve the threat.

Threat detectors have a clear sense of the efficiencies or inefficiencies of a system and how to manage through them. Detecting threats is about understanding an organization's position in the greater scheme of an industry and society. Conversely, threat detectors can also aid in uncovering a new way to add value to a business, and they do this by analysing new technology in the industry and the market in relation to the organization's position. Threat detectors are always looking for new ways to increase and improve the value of an organization by looking to improve what it offers to the market.

A simple realization that is crucial to the threat detector is that most technology consultants, tax accountants and lawyers do very well an atmosphere of Fear, Uncertainty and Doubt, or the 'FUD' factor. Recognizing this is key. The world is always in flux and is sometimes changing faster or in seemingly uncontrollable ways. Being able to recognize a threat—or an opportunity—ahead of time is what makes the threat detector crucial in an organization.

The Originator: as Cross-Pollinator

The Originator acts as a cross-pollinator. A cross-pollinator can apply ideas and concepts from technology to the real world and vice versa. They can identify real-world problems and figure out ways in which technology can help solve the problems. Conversely, they can analyse the system of logic that underpins different parts of life in the real world and use it to innovate new forms of technology. This can be something as simple as changing the way in which a technology functions to make it more efficient or even envisage a completely new type of technology. They can also understand the varied applicability of a technology and use it to solve a different problem than what it was originally devised for. Cross-pollinators can see the similarities and connections between seemingly unrelated fields of life and find ways to bridge that gap.

For example, while e-commerce has set off a huge boom in logistics and customer delivery supply chains, there is yet no worthwhile technology to efficiently manage customer returns at an e-commerce level. This problem is even greater for electronic items such as mobile phones, which must be manually inspected and graded when a customer returns them.

Interestingly, however, excellent technology in the form of robots, programmed cameras and the like already exist for quality control in manufacturing systems. These quality control systems work before a mobile phone leaves the plant, but not after. Manufacturing technology and customer care technology (the latter handles issues such as customer complaints and returns) aren't traditionally seen in the same light.

This begs the question: could aspects of these automated quality control technologies be used by a physical store or an e-commerce player when the supply chain works in reverse and phones, or other returned items, need to be sent back to the manufacturer?

There are several such examples but coming up with each of these ideas needs someone who truly understands how a business functions and can think laterally to bring in examples from other businesses to enhance their own business goals. The world is more interconnected than we think—this is since society tends to categorize and label things as if they are mutually exclusive. Cross-pollinators understand that this is just not true, and they see the connection between various aspects/industries in society and find ways to apply such connections to technology or vice versa.

The Leader

Leadership is about having a vision and being able to get others to collaborate with you to work towards this vision. This means having an intimate understanding of what an organization does and how it serves a particular market need as well as being able to envision the path forward for this organization, which would necessarily require a certain amount of innovation or revamping.

Technology has a habit of rendering businesses, organizations and industries obsolete over time. Leaders are able to predict this and manoeuvre the business into new waters to enable it to stay afloat and relevant in the rapidly changing technological world.

Leaders are also able to look at the big picture in the sense of what the social and cultural consequences of certain technologies are, because socio-cultural forces do inform and mould the market. Leaders need to be able to understand the implications of new technology upon society and how this will inform and affect their businesses. Planning for the future means being at least one step ahead of it. Adapting to new technologies not only involves knowing how to use said technologies but also knowing how these technologies will change the playing field. Good leaders innately understand this and are thus able to keep their organizations in play.

The Empath: as Caregiver/Experience Designer and Storyteller

Empathy is an important aspect of being able to adapt to a rapidly changing world. The way in which technology changes society can be so drastic that the advantages of new technology overshadow the negative consequences or side effects. People can be so enamoured by the new-found capability that technology provides that they do not bother or actually cannot see the detrimental aspects to it all.

Empathy helps one make more holistic decisions when it comes to analysing, understanding and implementing new technology in one's life. This can be on a personal level or organizational level or even on an industrial level. Companies and industries can make decisions regarding new technology in the sole pursuit of profit without considering the other, possibly negative, effects of said technology on society in general. The ability to employ empathy is one aspect of being a Caregiver.

Designers are the people who put the audience/users first. These are the people who understand that technology has no value unless it is delivered into the hands of the user in an easily consumable manner. The user experience is paramount to ensuring a new technology develops and maintains popularity in a market/society in general. Even if a technology is better or more efficient than a competitor's, if it is too difficult for users to properly comprehend or use, then it will be dead in the water.

At the end of the day, technology only matters when it can be properly used to improve the quality of life. The experience of using a technology is one of the biggest and most important parts of its value to an organization, an industry and to society in general. One of the main effects of technology is how it can change the way in which society functions—this is accomplished by building a personal and easy relationship between a technology and its users.

I am not talking about people who are focused solely on the user interface of a technology. There are courses in user experience and design available aplenty, but these are meant for the people who put together the nuts and bolts of a technology. In other words, computer programmers. I refer here to people who understand, at a visceral level, what their audience wants.

The other aspect is knowing how to express the nuances of the value of new technology to individuals and organizations.

This communication is done by being able to tell a story about it. Storytellers are able to make an idea or a concept personal to the audience. People may not care about any issue until it becomes personal for them, and that is what storytellers do. By making these things personal, storytellers are able to make individuals think more deeply and with empathy regarding the consequences and effects of new technology on their lives. Organizations may not necessarily pay heed to any issues outside of profit but when society speaks up, that is when organizations are forced to reconsider their stance on such things. This is the power of a storyteller and every organization needs one in order to ensure that it makes more holistic decisions.

This book is based around observations as thought starters and, in some cases, as real-world examples of these roles. Each observation should make you sit back and think about your business from a different frame of reference. The aim of this book is that you should be able to pick it up and read just a few pages—which will make you informed enough to hold a knowledgeable conversation on the topic and fit it into your 'knowledge base' to apply at work.

Chapter 3

Become a TechImpostor!

We will always have new twists and turns in the development of technology. However, the COVID-19 pandemic has given a sudden turbo boost to all sorts of technology business models that were lacklustre twenty-four months ago. Or these are technologies that were already well developed but have received new attention due to their sheer ability to step into the void in a world that was facing uncharted waters during the pandemic. This is the right time to start reading a book about becoming techproof the only way most of us will ever be able to: by diving in head first, just as some of these new-world businesses have done.

I am not suggesting that we go off and become computer programmers. There is a better way of getting tech-ready and tech-proficient than learning how to write computer programming code.

We only need to understand the broad working and application of a technology to truly become techproof. So, it is critical to understand the actual businesses we are in and the models that will make them prosper or wither. And importantly, a thorough scan of our own capabilities—especially as human beings—will be the capstone of the arch through which we will enter the world of using technology effectively in our businesses without allowing it to disrupt us or our businesses.

Wherever I look online, I am bombarded with ads for courses by trained information technology specialists who promise to teach coding skills. Everyone seems to think that the pandemic has shifted the world firmly towards technology and digitization, and that the only businesses of the future would be technologically-enabled ones, or at least those that can quickly pivot themselves to a digital, remote delivery model. Displaced workers are signing on for these courses in droves, in the hope that a newly-minted certification from an online learning app or a 'massive open online course' will make them employable again. And then there are parents of schoolgoing children who seem intent on producing a Sundar Pichai or a Satya Nadella at home, even if not a Bill Gates or a Sergey Brin or a Larry Page.

In relatively private conversations (insofar as WhatsApp or other messaging applications are still private), I hear from parents of schoolgoing children who have been enrolled in such classes. Almost down to the last person, most of these are complaints about the quality of such classes. Many parents claim that these courses and the companies running them are frauds. They allege that they are rife with false marketing, aggressive sales, and use photos of computer greats such as Bill Gates without their express permission along with false claims of millions of downloads. This last bit causes a 'fear of missing out' (colloquially called FOMO) among parents of young children and also among workers who feel they are not tech-savvy enough to take on the new world.

Preying on the gullibility of displaced workers or worried parents is not hard. To start with, most of those who are in this class think that the world is a tough place, and that one needs to adapt to what is definitely going to be a watershed event (the COVID-19 pandemic) by retooling or upskilling oneself to meet new demands of the future. The tumultuous changes that are going on in the world have hastened the adoption of new technologies such as artificial intelligence, machine learning, blockchain and the Internet of Things.

The pandemic will also serve to speed up the use of automation and technology in a bid to reduce human-to-human contact across a variety of business functions. India's computer industry body NASSCOM even has a website devoted to future skills. But in my observation, those who trained in other disciplines before finding themselves in careers that required a deep knowledge of several types of technology have two sure-fire ways of making themselves future techproof. One is to truly understand how a given technology works at a macro level, and the second is to figure out how to adapt oneself to the changes it brings.

While this is probably an overly simplified explanation of a tough task, learning how to leverage technology does not demand that you become an expert programmer. In reality, it only needs the application of certain specific filters to truly understand a technology, so that one can play the role of a via media between a person with only a passing knowledge of that technology and someone who is so deep in its workings that he or she cannot understand its broader implications. This is an old consulting secret that is not freely shared even among consultants of the same firm since it allows those who are adept at it to gainfully occupy that middle ground for decades.

The first rule of understanding technology is to approach each new breakthrough in an attempt to understand all the nuances of the 'functionality' that the new technology offers—at the individual, group, industry and societal levels. All that functionality means is a translation—in simple English—of what the technology actually achieves. For instance, understanding what blockchain technology actually does (it removes the need for a central verifier of transactions such as a bank or a credit card clearing house) allows you to become fluent in extending that understanding to various levels of aggregation—from the individual to a firm or nation.

Once you understand the functionality of the technology, filling in the gaps around the technical minutiae of how it is delivered is a much easier task, and can be left to the ones who know how to write code.

The second is to internalize the gross logic of how and why the technology functions, and its logical design sequencing within the economic value chain of an industry. In other words, one will

Diagram 1

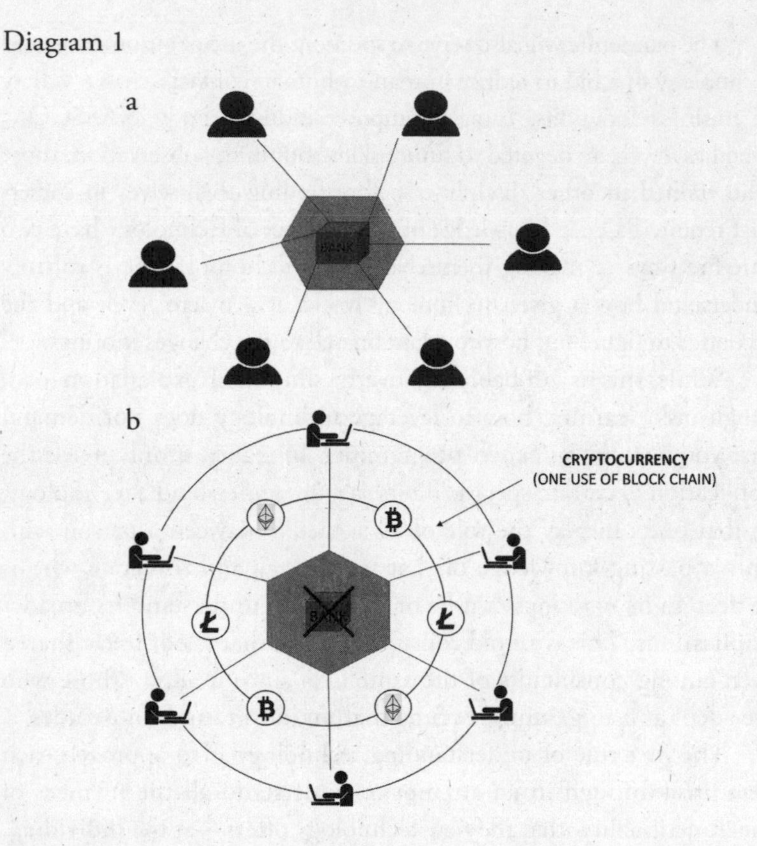

need to learn why the functionality of the technology one has now understood has economic impact. For example, blockchain could conceivably replace credit cards. The basis for this logic can come from a variety of areas: breaking existing trading groups, statistics to predict outcomes, user-friendly access and so on.

The third is to learn from where the technology gets its data or information on which it acts to provide the above-mentioned technical functionality. Once these three components are properly understood, one will then be armed with enough knowledge to see how to adapt to it, or better still, profit from it!

The genesis of the thought process for this book was the realization that any top tier strategy consultant only uses a simple set of methods, married with sound bites of information in order to seem as if he or she were an expert in technology or a specific area of business. The art lies in not getting too technical and losing your audience by throwing about too many acronyms, but in explaining it to them in a way that makes them understand the broad brushstrokes around what a certain technology can actually do for them. The consultant does that while simultaneously convincing them that he or she is the perfect person to convert the fable into reality for the organization or executive they are talking to.

In order to accomplish this, the consultant (usually unconsciously, but always from having watched masters at this act do so when they were young) puts on a role that he or she plays for the organization he is working for or selling to. They become 'TechImpostors'. This role varies based on whom they're speaking to and what they're speaking about, and fall by and large into a set of roles that we will discuss in this book.

Like many other consultants, I have lived this journey myself. In August 1994, I found myself working for a pioneer firm in artificial intelligence. About five years prior, I had gone to work for Xerox in what used to be the company's headquarters in Rochester, New York. I was straight out of MBA school, and picked up another master's in economics, studying part-time while at Xerox. I was by no means a technologist and had only a passing familiarity with computers. Xerox was a behemoth in those years, and by shifting into a small technology firm in 1994 instead, I was taking one of the greatest risks of my life. Most Xerox long-timers warned me that I was making a mistake that I would regret for a lifetime.

I wasn't expecting to make a switch into the technology field at all. And certainly not into artificial intelligence, which in those years was an esoteric corner of information technology. The Carnegie Group, an offshoot of the AI labs at Carnegie Mellon University, hired both my wife and me to work for the firm in its Denver office. This office was set up to service the telecom giant US WEST, one of the owners of the Carnegie Group. My wife was a software telecom engineer, and her technical skills were of more direct interest to Carnegie than mine.

I, on the other hand, came with next to zero technology capability, but a solid view of the intricacies of how large businesses worked, since I had spent the preceding years working for Xerox's elite Corporate Audit and Operational Analysis group or CA&OA, as it was then known through the company. CA&OA was formed to act as an internal consulting group for Xerox and was an extremely powerful force within the firm. In those years, Xerox was something of a conglomerate, with interests in business products, computing, (pre-web) networking, imaging, as also in financial services such as investment banking, insurance and mutual funds. It also housed the famed Palo Alto Research Center or PARC, the original genesis of many inventions we take for granted today, such as windows-based computing, distributed computing, email and digital printing.

The CA&OA group was similar to the elite Audit department at GE, also then a successful conglomerate with varied business areas. These groups met often to benchmark and use each other's ideas for acting as an elite consulting group within their respective firms. CA&OA was staffed by mid-career executives who were on the fast track and who already had between ten and twenty years of business experience in their own speciality areas such as engineering, information technology (IT), product development, manufacturing, sales, marketing and services. A tour of duty through CA&OA virtually guaranteed a quick and highly coveted progression to the senior management ranks, complete with corner office and wooden furniture within a few months of transferring from the department. I was the only fresh MBA hired by CA&OA in that year, for reasons that I can attribute to nothing but sheer good fortune.

The work was intellectually very challenging and required extensive travel. I was handed plane tickets on my first day at work and told to prepare myself for a six-month-long exhaustive review of Xerox's services business, which was responsible for the maintenance of all Xerox's equipment installed at customer sites. Xerox Services had over 15,000 service representatives covering the length and breadth of the US and Canada. It also had about 650 phone centre representatives in five time zones, whose sole function was to take calls from customers requesting service or repair of their installed machines. They also, in turn, dispatched their 15,000 repair engineer colleagues to those customer sites, while taking the customer location, the machine type, the rep's location vis-à-vis the customer at the time the field service rep called in to be dispatched to their next call. In addition, this function matched the field rep's training and capabilities with the repair job that needed to be performed, since Xerox's installed base of machines included everything from simple desktop photocopiers to extremely sophisticated enterprise class electronic business printers used for such functions as printing credit card bills or bank statements that needed to be mailed out periodically.

At the heart of all this was an IT system called Field Work Support System or FWSS, which had been written by Xerox's own IT department and which was an incredibly sophisticated computer program combining logistics, queueing theory, inventory management for spare parts, as well as geographic locations and travel times in order to get the right rep with the right parts to the customer within a pre-agreed time, and who could finish the job within the standard Mean Time to Repair or MTR for that type of equipment. Suffice to say that the only way I could participate in the review of the services operation was to quickly familiarize myself with the functional ins and outs of FWSS—which meant sitting in front of 'green-screen' age mainframe computer screens to parse out what was actually going on in the field.

FWSS was written in COBOL (short for COmmon Business Oriented Language), a programming language made popular in the 1970s by IBM (one of my later employers), which was designed to work on IBM mainframe computers. I didn't know a word of COBOL then—and I still don't. But I certainly picked up all the nuances of what the program actually did along with its sophisticated mathematical modelling for inventory, queuing and routing of reps to customer locations based on their relative geographical proximity and skill level.

This was the first of many such reviews. In a few short years, I had seen everything—manufacturing, sales, accounting, payables, receivables, supplies and multilingual billing in French and English for Xerox's customers in French Canada (Montreal and Quebec). I also worked on the team that sold off Furman-Selz, a specialist Wall Street investment bank that was fully owned by Xerox.

My next job at Xerox was in Incentive Strategy—the group that set and changed commissions monthly for 12,000 field sales representatives that Xerox had across North America. I can safely say that within a few short months, I learned more about how to influence human behaviour by affecting an individual's earnings that even a degree in Human Resources could have taught me. This was to be my last assignment at Xerox before I moved to sunny Denver to work for the Carnegie Group.

The hiring managers at Carnegie Group, Ted Smith and Arvind Sathi, knew my wife and I were a joint package. Arvind was a highly regarded PhD in artificial intelligence from Carnegie Mellon University and, to this day, I thank my stars that he and Ted realized that I had an uncommon ability to break down businesses into their piece part components and then reassemble the components all over again in a different and hopefully more efficient manner. He created a role for me as a 'pre-sales business analyst'. The idea was that I would be able to break down business problems into bite-sized pieces that the firm's customers would agree to invite the Carnegie Group to solve. My work after each successful sale that I led or participated in was to logically put together these business components in a novel and more efficient way, so that these could be used as specifications by the firm's computer programmers to write programming code to fulfil.

By the end of 1994, I found myself writing object-oriented programming specifications in Birmingham, Alabama for the enterprise sales organization of BellSouth. Here, I need to make an important point. I wasn't writing the computer programming code; instead, I was providing programmers who would write the computer programs the actual functional specifications of what their code would need to execute. BellSouth was hoping the AI project would provide a boost to sales of its 'Centrex' equipment. Centrex was a very sophisticated electronic sub telephone exchange that could be used by medium to very large-scale customers who were outsourcing their entire voice telecom needs to BellSouth.

Now, over twenty-seven years later, I have spent more than 90 per cent of my career in technology. Along the way, I have learnt how specific business verticals such as telecom and financial services work, learnt how to understand the functionality and structure of all manner of computer programs, and how to deliver large-scale IT projects focused on software products and services. I have also spent time negotiating some of the largest and most difficult deals in technology outsourcing and in consulting on technology strategy with some of the finest companies in the world. I have lost count of the number of right turns I have made from a career perspective, but I can attest that each one left me better and more informed, after I got over being petrified by the sudden change!

People also assume that there is another key, a behavioural one, that several self-help books tout. However, many of these books, some of them timeless classics, do not provide any practical advice with respect to learning technology or indeed on how to move along with its never-ceasing changes. I will delve into some of these aspects later in this book, but only as simple, practical advice that anyone could use. I make no claims of being an expert in mental health or behavioural science; all I can do in these parts of the book is show you the simple tools I have used that have worked well for me. Try them if you like, but if you have a toolkit for self-improvement of your mental status that you think works better for you, then go right ahead and use your toolkit instead.

Also, it is time we stopped trying to fix ourselves by looking solely to the insights of behavioural science to help us form new behaviours or preparing for the future or by merely learning how to write computer code, while completely ignoring how the pieces of the jigsaw actually fit together.

Chapter 4

Understanding Business Process—a Simple Key

While both a personality self-assessment and some ability with computers is necessary for people who would make the leap into technology, the missing piece has always been understanding the functional aspects of computing.

By functional aspects, I mean questions like:

Which exact business task does the computer program perform?

Why is this task particularly important to this department or facet of the business?

Does this task directly impact the overall business or is it just a peripheral activity?

Whose head would roll if this business task were done sloppily?

Do customers care about this task?

Do other people who contract with the business (suppliers, contractors, third party distributors, dealers) care about this task? If they don't care, would making them care be better for my business?

Does the government care about this task?

And most important: could one do without this task?

In order to be able to answer these questions, you need a framework for thinking—a cheat sheet if you will, for how to quickly assess a business function. So here I want to share probably the most important construct one can ever have with respect to understanding a business function correctly, and to assess whether or not that function is in fact performing as it should. The more you apply this construct, the better you get at analysing business functions and understanding the role technology could potentially play in making that function more precise, more efficient, or even in eliminating it altogether. Here, I must thank David Burton, my first boss at Xerox, who, along with my senior colleagues Joe Modugno, Rene Manrique and Dominic Montulli, made sure I had a rock-solid understanding of business process functionality. So here is the magic construct. *If there is nothing else you take away from this book except burn these five principles into your memory, the book would have achieved its goal:*

The Problem: A problem is simply a deviation from expectations. For example, if you expect that a set of business processes will produce exactly the same result 99 per cent of the time, but in actuality the set only produces the same result 90 per cent of the time, you have a problem. Simply stated, there is a deviation from expectations of 99 per cent accuracy.

In this context, I am left with no option but to use a time-worn phrase to point out something that should be obvious and that many people parrot: 'Problems can also be seen as opportunities.' While this is true, I would strongly suggest you use the 'deviation from expectations' method to assess and define opportunities as well, without which you are likely not to be taken seriously, especially if you are taking on a role where you would like to spearhead or facilitate a change in your organization's normal way of working. Analytically pinpointing the fact that current practices and processes do not meet current or future expectations (without apportioning blame on to an individual or group) is a sure-fire way to get you noticed as a forward-looking strategic thinker.

The Cause: Every problem has a cause. This could be due to a large variety of contributing factors, but it is up to you to figure out which exact one is the cause. You might have workers who don't adhere to a process that was well defined in the beginning, or even a process that wasn't designed right in the first place. This is where your judgement, experience, powers of observation and reading books like this one come in.

The Evidence: You cannot claim a problem exists without first providing evidence that it does. This is all about quantifying or otherwise proving that the problem exists. For instance, in the problem statement above, the 9 per cent deviation would have to be established conclusively. For this, you might use a variety of methods—measurement of the accuracy of a sample of the outputs from the process, or the number of times the process needs to be escalated to someone with greater skills so that it can be concluded. The key here is that the evidence needs to be quantified. This doesn't mean that you need higher order mathematics or hard data to prove it; it simply means that you can state with relative certainty—even if that certainty has only been established by interviewing people who perform the process or receive its output—that a quantifiable deviation from expectations exists.

The Impact: Any problem deviation from expectations must have an impact. And yes, so must every opportunity. These can be soft as well as hard impacts, but again, you need to be able to state the case either quantifiably, or monetarily, or otherwise demonstrate conclusively that the deviation from expectations is causing a clear business impact. No impact simply means that there is no problem. Or no opportunity.

The Recommendation: This is simply the obverse of the cause. You recommend actions that remove the cause. This could be as simple as additional training. It could also mean the computerization and automation of the process. Or outsourcing the handling of the process to an external organization to accomplish. Regardless of what the recommendation is, it must directly erase the cause, otherwise it is of no use to the business.

Diagram 2

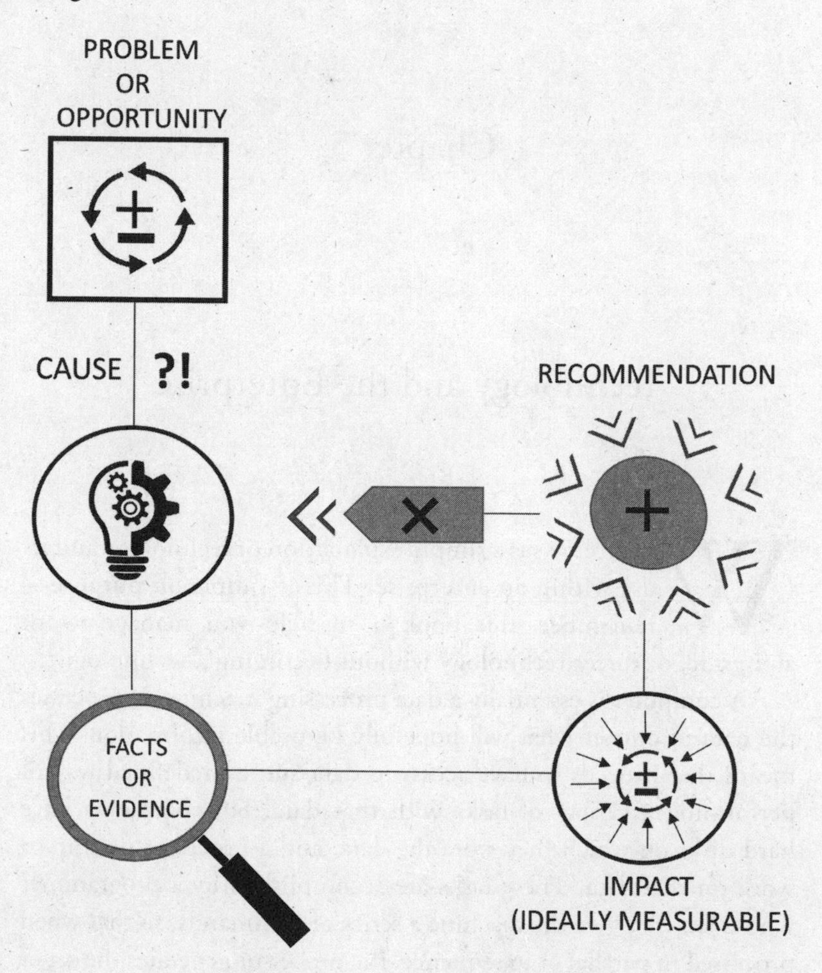

There are obvious limitations to this method. Please do not try to use it in areas such as medicine, unless you are a doctor, of course.

Chapter 5

Technology and the Enterprise

What follows is a simple explanation of technology and its use within an enterprise. This is simple on purpose—remember, this book is to help you manage, work alongside, or direct technology without becoming a technologist.

A computer is essentially a data processing machine. It processes the data to output what will hopefully be usable information. This means that it needs to have access to data and a predefined way of performing a variety of tasks with that data. So, computers have hard disks on which they store the data, and a processor or chip to work on that data. These tasks are accomplished by a programmer whose job is to give the machine a series of commands, so that when processed in parallel or in sequence, the processor generates the set of information that the programmer desires from the large databank it has on its hard disk.

Moreover, most computers, especially in a business environment, don't work as stand-alone machines. They are connected to one another in a 'network' so that, say, a first computer can query the data that is resident, say, on a second computer and process it on its own processor. For the most part, this interconnected set of computers is what forms the Internet. So, when you do, say, a Google search on your computer or phone (phones are also computers these days), it connects to Google's vast network of machines that houses data and applies the query. Once the right computer that houses the specific data or information you are looking for is found, your query then runs on the remote computer which then responds with your answer, using the network to reach you. What enables this is that your basic query is then converted into a program that the Google computer can understand, and it is this program that massages numbers and sifts through this data to fulfil your query.

But the world of computing is far more complex than just running a query. As it gets more complex (as in, say, a large company), there are many functions that require data to be processed and for the information that comes out of that processing to be used in a specific way for the function to work accurately. This means that the computer programs written so that this function can be performed need to make focused calls for exact types of data that are resident either in a specific database or on a distributed set of computers. The programs then need to manipulate this data in a specific way—by assigning the data to certain individuals, for instance, or by performing a mathematical function such as multiplying or adding the data together. All the calls and operations need to be exactly coordinated so that the integrity of the function is preserved. Even with all the computing capacity in the world, the computing function may still perform the task accurately, but will completely miss the target if it is not coordinated accurately or if it picks up irrelevant data.

Let's take payables, for instance. This is the business function that makes sure a company's suppliers are paid in time for their services or products, or that the bank loans they have taken are paid off in correct instalments, among other payments that the company may need to make in the normal course of running its business. This department usually reports to the CFO, either through the controller of the company or through its treasurer.

For this function to work properly, it usually requires the data from an invoice (or other document that sets off a payment obligation) to go through a sequence of steps so that the data is accurately captured and then processed. Let's say Company Y sends an invoice to your company. Or that the first document itself was sent some time ago—but required periodic payments over several months or years, as in a loan payback. The data from this document is first captured. This, for the most part, is done by an individual human who keys in the data from the invoice. This is the first pair of eyes, the data entry operator, who looks at the invoice and keys in the data. In some cases, a human is not needed since the computer program already has the invoice in its storage, and all it has to do is to compare the amount payable on the invoice with the master data in the payables file. Note that this bit of automation may have eliminated part of the work of the first pair of eyes, but companies are usually careful enough to make sure that the automation only works for low dollar amounts. High dollar amounts will still need manual intervention. This is called the 'Maker' part of the process.

Next, the data needs to be processed for accuracy by comparing it with the data in a master file that shows all your company's payments due. At this point, a Request for Manual Assistance (or RMA) stops the process. Here, a second human (the second pair of eyes) looks at the data that has been entered and certifies that it is correct and complete. Then, the computer program designed and developed for the payables function routes the transaction further up the chain, to an 'approver' or the third set of manual eyes that looks at the proposed transaction and instructs the computer to process the payment. At this point, the computer program picks up and communicates with other computer programs that cut the cheque or process the electronic payment via the company's banks.

All this may sound simple enough in practice, and it usually is, but things can and do go awry. On 11 August 2020, Citi was set to transfer $8 million to lenders of cosmetics company Revlon in its capacity as a loan agent. There were 'six eyes' at hand to make sure everything went without a hitch. Of the three, two were in India. The two worked with an Indian technology partner of Citi.

Oops! The trio—the third person was a senior Citi manager—mistakenly paid Revlon's lenders around $900 million. The incident—billed as the biggest blunder in banking history—expectedly made global headlines. It was back in the news in February 2021 when Citigroup lost a legal battle in the US to recover the money it accidentally transferred. News on the original overpayment and the ensuing legal wrangles after the snafu have been covered by various news sources, including a report in the *Wall Street Journal* that appeared on 13 August 2020.

There are several lessons here. First, no computer system is capable of taking away human interfaces completely. Second, the actual business function, and every possible error condition that can be generated either by the computer systems or by the humans handling them, needs to be completely understood with respect to the actual function that the business is trying to execute. And third, a deep understanding of how the overall process actually functions and what impact it can have on a business is a critical part of any executive's arsenal, especially if he or she expects to be effective in their careers.

In a statement broadly issued to the press after the incident, Citibank said, 'As a result of a review undertaken last year (2019), we are in the process of upgrading our loan operations platform. We take pride in the role that we play as a global leader in financial services and recognize that an operational error of this nature is unacceptable. We have put significant, additional controls in place until the new system is operational.'

While tasks, whether or not they need continuous learning, can be automated, one thing a soulless machine can never have is living consciousness.

The Carnegie Group, the company I worked for two and a half decades ago, was an offshoot of Carnegie Mellon University's

Artificial Intelligence (AI) Laboratories. That company is long gone. Today, a think-tank goes by the same name. While it was still in existence, the original Carnegie Group worked on some of the most cutting-edge AI products of its time. It was funded by a consortium of firms such as Caterpillar and US WEST (now Qwest Corp.) and its sole aim was to look for the application of AI technologies in businesses. My boss, Arvind Sathi, now an IBM scientist, received his PhD under AI pioneer Herbert Simon, a Nobel laureate who was a professor at Carnegie Mellon.

After some years of doing cutting-edge work in fields such as multilingual billing (translating complex telecom company bills into both English and Spanish) or adding 'intelligence' through the use of 'heuristics' or rules of thumb that allowed computer programs to grow in learning as they matured in use, the Carnegie Group became a victim of that most commercial of all drivers—earnings—and had to shift to plain vanilla IT services. It then simply got acquired.

* * *

An ideal intelligent computer program can change itself to take actions that maximize its chance of success at performing a task. According to computer scientists Stuart Russell and Peter Norvig, the term 'artificial intelligence' is applied when a machine mimics 'cognitive' functions that humans associate with other human minds, such as 'learning' and 'problem-solving'. Simply put, the computer ceases to be a machine that simply carries out instructions based on computer programs. It gains the ability to recognize, learn and see patterns such as a consumer's buying behaviour as well as to analyse and solve problems such as finding the shortest way to the nearest petrol pump or restaurant on its own, with no new programs needing to be written. In essence, the computer system writes extensions to its own original programs that make it more efficient at new tasks when it processes through the data thrown at it as it is used.

Contrast this with process automation—robotic or otherwise—which takes manual tasks that do not need much learning and simply mechanizes them. This could be as simple as the scanning of invoices to be processed in an accounts payable system. All the programmer has to do is define where fields such as amount due and payment address show up on the invoice, and then program the system to look in those particular spots to find this information. This step then becomes automated and removes the need for a manual keyboard operator to input such information on to the system, thereby displacing these keyboard operators. This kind of programming is not AI.

Most IT services firms selfishly blur the line between process automation and AI. Despite their best efforts at obfuscation, the line is really clear. Automation simply mechanizes routine tasks. But in AI, the computer program itself learns as it goes along, creating a database of information that it then uses rules of thumb to analyse. In a vital twist that has occurred in machine learning in the past few months, these databases themselves generate additional computer programming code as they learn more, without the need for an army of computer programmers. In AI speak, this is now often referred to as 'deep learning'.

As AI becomes more capable, it simply is no longer considered 'intelligent'. For example, the multilingual work I used to do over two decades ago is no longer called AI since it is now routine. So will it be with many of the programs now considered to be on the cutting edge of AI.

What is not in doubt, however, is that automation—whether routine or 'intelligent'—will lead to seismic shifts in employment, especially in India with its armies of programmers, and much like the industrial revolution in the 1800s in the West. People spinning or weaving fabrics lost their jobs after Eli Whitney invented the cotton gin in 1794, as did many a buggy-whip maker after Karl Benz invented the automobile as we know it in 1885, and several bank cashiers after the ATM was invented. History—and classical economics—has proven time and again that a revolution such as this simply changes the nature of human work in the long term (after the excruciatingly painful short-term effects of job displacement have worked themselves out). Stop suggesting computer programming as a future profession to your children, unless you're sure they will be genius scientists.

Simon, Tom McCarthy and others founded the AI field on the claim that human intelligence 'can be so precisely described that a machine can be made to simulate it'. This raises questions about the ethics of creating artificial beings endowed with human-like intelligence. It is not just programmers who will lose jobs to AI, but also pilots, machinists, journalists and others. Elon Musk, himself a heavy investor in AI, says, 'With artificial intelligence, we are summoning the demon.'

This requires a quick foray into metaphysics to debunk. While tasks, whether or not they need continuous learning, can be automated, there is one thing that a soulless machine can never do, and that is to have living consciousness. Computer programs can be taught tricks that involve the application of learning, just as apes, dogs and humans can, but learning is not intelligence. Living consciousness is the key to all true cognition. Explaining 'consciousness' is something that every spiritual scripture has tried to address, and the world has no shortage of such scriptures. But for now, we can make do with the simple definition that says consciousness is the simple act of knowing that you are alive.

If you doubt me, then simply ask yourself who is listening to these words as you read them to yourself. Is it your learning neurons—or some other, larger field of consciousness into which words and thoughts like these come and go and are understood? Next, go ahead and ask yourself whether you will lose your job to AI—and watch your mind (your learning repository database) respond. Both the question and your answer to it, whether driven by the limbic response of fear or by the intelligent reasoning of your database, are perceived by the real living consciousness in you. And unlike learning, it is this consciousness that is the root of true cognition. Only sentient beings have it. Even apes and dogs have it, though to a lesser degree than us; a computer program automatically generating lines of code so that it can make itself more efficient does not.

Section II

Chapter 6

How Modern Business Function Processes Evolved

Before I move on to giving you information to help with each role you can play within your company, it would serve us to go down memory lane to understand how the inter-workings between business processes and technology have been changing over the years.

The first person who saw this with clarity during the industrial age was Frederick W. Taylor. Taylor was an American mechanical engineer who became widely known for his work in increasing industrial efficiency. In my opinion, he was the father of management consulting. In 1911, Taylor summed up his efficiency techniques in his book *The Principles of Scientific Management* that was published by Harper and Brothers and was a 144-page treatise dedicated solely to Taylor's views on how management worked. In 2001, Fellows of the Academy of Management voted Taylor's book as the most influential management book of the twentieth century. His pioneering work in applying engineering principles to the work done on the factory floor was instrumental in the creation and development of the branch of engineering that is now known as industrial engineering. Taylor made his name in scientific management and in the meanwhile, however, made his fortune coming up with patents that improved the processing of steel.

Taylor had done well enough academically to be admitted to Harvard University, and in fact passed its qualifying examination with flying colours, but allegedly his poor eyesight made him take up an industrial apprentice job instead. Early in his career on the shop floor, Taylor recognized that workmen were not working their machines, or themselves, nearly as hard as they could and that this resulted in high labour costs for the company. When he became a foreman, he expected more output from his workmen. In order to determine how much work should properly be expected, he began to study and analyse the productivity of both the men and the machines. Taylor labelled his focus on the human component of production 'scientific management'. Time and motion studies—or studies of how long it took a focused worker to do a particular task—and then setting productivity measures around the initial measurements was one of the hallmarks of such work.

For many years, Taylor remained the gold standard. In some of his thirty-nine books and a ten-year series of columns for the *Wall Street Journal*, the management guru Peter Drucker said that Taylor was the first man in recorded history who deemed work deserving of systematic observation and study. On Taylor's scientific management rests, above all, the tremendous surge of affluence in the last seventy-five years, which has lifted the working masses in the developed countries well above any level recorded before, even for the well-to-do. Taylor, though the Isaac Newton (or perhaps the Archimedes) of the science of work, laid only its first foundations, however. In 1975, Drucker is supposed to have written of Taylor that not much had been added to his work by management theorists since Taylor had died in 1915.

This was certainly still true when Xerox's Field Work Support System, which I wrote of in a previous chapter, was designed. It based its queuing and routing algorithms on studies of how long it would take a service representative to repair a machine or to perform routine maintenance tasks on it, and routed the service representative to the next call based on a mean (or average) time to repair, called MTR in the company's jargon. Service representatives were expected to meet their MTR commitments, and the study I participated in looked at ways to reduce MTR in order to increase productivity in the field. This again included time and motion studies in order to benchmark the best possible MTR on a class of machine and changing service representatives' incentives so they would push for ever-lower MTR performance.

A later version of the systems that managed the field workforce focused on what pieces of the human dispatcher's job could be automated. Xerox issued its service representatives electronic 'bricks'—a sort of one-trick-pony version of today's pagers or cellular phones that only displayed the next few calls in the queue, and allowed the service representative to pick their next destination on their own without having to rely on a call to the dispatch centre and a conversation with a dispatcher who was interacting with the actual system. Most of the IT being applied even in those days was to automate routine tasks that could conceivably be better performed by a computer or by a piece of hardware with direct ties to a computer system.

Examples of Taylorism in modern corporations still abound. Most industry watchers are talking about the need for IT services companies to become more product-focused and less people- and services-focused, thereby creating 'non-linear' revenue models for themselves. This, in the wake of massive advances in technology and a steep drop in the cost of providing these technologies to billions of people through the Internet. Robots, they say, are now capable of doing the work of humans and that process automation through technology will cause several Indian IT programmers to lose their jobs.

But every cloud has a silver lining. The Internet of Things (IoT) presents a massive opportunity to IT services providers who don't want to—or can't—move away from a people-centric model. Many recent studies by Gartner and other analyst firms promise that IoT will be the next wave of technology taking over the world.

Interestingly, however, many of these analysts are also tempering expectations by saying that IoT is not for everyone and that its uptake in certain industries will be significantly lower than in other ones. As late as five years ago, they also claimed that less than 40 per cent of global CEOs even know what IoT means.

I don't see this as being a problem. The cost of technology and bandwidth are both always dropping, and soon the IoT wave will become a deluge. If IoT takes off, just as new technologies often do (even if they're not always better technologies than the ones they replace), the IoT hype can make for hefty IT services revenues for India's IT sector.

I will digress just enough to provide a simple definition to ease the reader's understanding. IoT simply means that many more of the devices and 'things' you use every day will become inexorably linked to the Internet and therefore to the various IT systems owned by the companies that first built these things, so that these companies can now monitor how you use their things and make 'helpful' suggestions. Your washing machine is such a 'thing', just like your iron, your car, your refrigerator, your fitness monitor bracelet, and maybe even your e-cigarette. What this means is that there will be some level of computing power in each of these things, and that each of these things will in turn be connected to the Internet—either through a telecom services provider—or your home Wi-Fi.

The possibilities are endless. A febrile imagination can dream up all sorts of uses. Your refrigerator notices that you're running low on milk, informs a giant computer somewhere up in the sky (oh, sorry—the cloud) and voila, your phone talks to you and tells you to stop at the grocery store on your way home from work so that your breakfast tomorrow can include a good old Indian chai rather than black tea. Take this a step further—the refrigerator informs the neighbourhood grocery store and the 'doodh-walla' is at your doorstep in a trice.

IoT is not new. This sort of stuff has been tried for decades—and it's intrusive. When I worked for Xerox—long before Netscape brought the Web to the world in a graphical user interface—the company made much of its 'Remote Interactive Communications' (RIC) module, which was standard equipment on its high-volume photocopying machines. This module, which needed its own dedicated phone line, sensed when something was about to go wrong with your copier—and let Xerox's central customer repair and service systems know that something was about to go awry before it actually did—thereby causing a Xerox service rep to arrive at your door demanding to service your machine when it hadn't broken down. This was a source of great annoyance to the secretary who was trying to get multiple copies of a document xeroxed and bound in time for the boss's meeting in the next hour. Little wonder that RIC calls soon got relegated to a false alarm status and were routinely ignored by Xerox's 15,000-person US service force. And I certainly don't want my refrigerator's manufacturer knowing the contents of my fridge (in which I happen to be conducting an advanced chemistry experiment on how long I can keep a coconut chutney fresh).

But it's just this sort of thing that is heaven-sent for an IT services provider. You first charge a hefty sum to build bespoke and custom solutions for refrigerator RICs, washing machine RICs, toaster RICs and car RICs, and then charge again for constantly tweaking and redefining their systems as clients continually bring out new models of their 'things' or their end customers change their use patterns and demand more privacy—or finally in desperation, cut off the Internet connection to the thing—much like harried secretaries all over the US pulled out the phone lines from their Xerox copiers, preferring instead to call for service when the thing was actually broken. As a wag once said, the only thing that is getting more expensive in IT is the people.

Chapter 7

How A Business Process Based on Old Thought Made Its Way into the Tech Revolution

Taylorism has also taken on an ugly tone in the modern 'gig economy'. Companies that manage their workers through a mathematical scheduling algorithm are new economy darlings—the Ubers, Swiggys and Dunzos of this world are a great example.

Prevailing thinking seems to indicate that email-shuffling middle managers, who do little but route work to underlings and suck up to the layer above, will soon be without a job. Super-efficient queuing theory-based algorithms such as those used by web-based businesses such as Uber, Lyft, Ola and restaurant delivery/courier websites will soon take over the function of efficiently allocating work in many other services-based organizations.

For instance, in a company that plots employees on a bell curve in terms of performance and weeds out stragglers, an algorithm can now handle the emotionally difficult aspects of the task.

Let's examine taxi scheduling and courier services. Drivers for taxi-scheduling apps are 'small business owners' who choose when they come to work, but once they are working, are subject to strict algorithm-driven control. They are only given a few seconds to respond to a ride request routed by the app and are not told the customer's final destination until they have picked them up. If the drivers miss a certain number of requests, they are automatically logged out of their smartphones for a set amount of time, much like a penalty box where they are unable to see and respond to ride requests. They are subject to an instant feedback mechanism where the passenger rates the driver and his or her vehicle. These ratings are monitored, and taxi-scheduling apps can deactivate drivers should their ratings fall below a certain threshold.

In cases like these, the small business owners (the hundreds of thousands of drivers all over the world who drive for Uber, Lyft, Ola and others) never actually see a human being from the company for which they work. Their entire contact with the firm is limited to the app on their smartphones that links them to the taxi-hailing business. They are, in effect, working for a robot—a computer program. This program is ruthlessly efficient and is devoid of feelings. If the numbers don't add up, you are out.

In the new-age marketplaces, none of this is considered an employee-to-employer relationship. The drivers, who are small business owners, simply contract with the computer program at the taxi-hailing firm. As Joseph Campbell said: 'Computers are like Old Testament gods; lots of rules and no mercy.' And therein lies the rub. If a worker is not an employee, then how does one fault a marketplace organization for predatory practices?

We might see trade unions soon at a variety of services enterprises, in an attempt to 'humanize' the relentless algorithms of these computer programs.

Uber, for instance, is in talks with drivers in the US over a dispute on whether they are to be considered employees. And there are cases being brought by unions against firms such as Uber at employment tribunals in the UK. The UK's Supreme Court has recently sided with Uber's drivers who filed suit and declared that they are in fact employees. The Court has referred the matter to the employment tribunal to draft necessary policy (Uber BV and Others vs Aslam, Farrar and Others, case number 2202550/2015 and others).

Some time ago, during the US presidential election, Uber and other gig-economy firms had won a big legal victory in California. During a presidential election, other referendum choices are also on the ballot in each state. California carried a referendum in the 2020 election on a yes/no vote on a measure named Proposition 22. It was critically important to firms such as Uber, Lyft, DoorDash and GrubHub. These businesses that use 'casual' workers had threatened to leave the state had the measure not been voted in. They wanted their drivers and food deliverers classified as contractors and not as employees.

They have become a part of our day-to-day life and been valued in the private equity world as well as public markets at tens of billions of dollars, but gig economy companies operate on precarious business models. For example, ride-hailing or delivery companies such as Uber and Lyft often lose money on every delivery made and every ride given. In other words, their 'unit-economics' are such that they are losing money as companies for each transaction they undertake. Uber's loss before interest and tax was $625 million in 2020's third quarter. Over the 2020 financial year, its net loss was $6.8 billion. A lot of this has been attributed to the pandemic. Such companies have signalled that they can turn profitable as soon as the administration of COVID-19 vaccines helps reopen economies across the world.

But running a profitable business needs a company to both attract new revenue as the pandemic recedes as well as keep its costs down. Employee classification would have given rise to a slew of labour rights that today's gig workers, as 'independent contractors', do not enjoy. It would therefore have raised costs for gig economy firms, which, in the face of the pandemic-induced decline in revenues, would mean that their expectations of turning a corner to profitability would have received a jolt.

Workers for gig companies in California will not have the same rights as other employees to paid sick days, overtime pay, unemployment insurance or a workplace covered by occupational safety and health laws. California's Assembly had tried to head this off earlier with a law of its own called Assembly Bill 5 (AB5), which would have guaranteed these rights. According to the *Los Angeles Times*, one lawmaker, who wrote AB5 and opposed Proposition 22, said: 'Instead of paying their drivers, gig corporations forged a deceptive $204-million campaign to change the rules for themselves and provide their workers with less than our state laws require.'

After spending over $200 million in California, Uber and other gig companies managed, through slick marketing, to convince the state's otherwise left-leaning electorate that they were actually going to pay their drivers and delivery agents well. But according to the National Employment Law Project (NELP), the truth was that someone driving an average of 35 km every hour in a 40-hour workweek would make $287 less per week after Proposition 22 passed. This is in addition to a slew of healthcare and other reductions. The NELP said a 'permanent underclass of workers has been created'.

Uber has faced its share of legal troubles outside the US. It conceded defeat in China and sold out to Didi Chuxing, its largest competitor there. It has also been facing flak in Europe and the UK. In France, Uber lost a decision at the country's top court last year, meaning that its drivers had the right to be considered employees. In other parts of Europe, such as Germany, Italy and Spain, Uber's labour practices have raised the hackles of local taxi unions, which have so far been able to convince lawmakers to limit its availability.

But beguiling an electorate into making a convenient choice, itself a gargantuan effort, would seem to be easier than convincing justices of supreme courts. In a continuance of Uber BV and Others vs Aslam, Farrar and Others (case number 2202550/2015 and others), Uber suffered a major defeat in Britain, one of its most important markets, when that country's Supreme Court said a group of drivers should be classified as workers entitled to a minimum wage and vacation time. The British Supreme Court justices ruled unanimously that Uber behaved more like an employer by setting rates, assigning rides, requiring drivers to follow certain routes, and using a rating system to discipline them, though it claimed it was only a technology platform that connected drivers with passengers. For now, this decision is limited only to the twenty-five drivers who originally brought the case. The ruling will be relayed to an employment tribunal to determine how it will affect all Uber drivers in Britain.

Unsurprisingly, Uber is playing down the court's decision, saying it will press the employment tribunal to limit the ruling's scope. However, anyone with a basic sense of logic can see how this would cascade down to the 60,000-plus Uber drivers in Britain and reverberate well beyond that country's borders. Its impact will also go beyond Uber to other gig economy firms that rely heavily on casual workers.

In India, we are somewhat isolated from such issues. Our disposition towards 'informal economy' workers has had laissez-faire attitudes. It's thus a surprise to see an attempt at ensuring that food delivery agents and ride-hailing drivers get some social security benefits under a revised labour code. How gig employers will resist this in India remains unknown.

As a student, I had often wondered how autorickshaw drivers in Bengaluru had extremely strong unions and could call a wildcat strike and bring life to a halt in the city. This was even more wondrous given that the drivers were themselves not employees of any firm—the vast majority of them rented their autorickshaws for a set fee every day—and ran their own small businesses.

The sociological impact of working for an algorithm is unquestionable. Interestingly, this impact will loosely follow work orders originally established by middle management for efficient production at factories. Except, this time it is the algorithm allocating work, and not the middle manager. Workers are bound to fight back and organize into unions and or litigious groups, and politicians will definitely interfere. Meanwhile, muddled middle managers will be mechanized and will go off to either be retrained or to retire.

Until now, we have seen the rise of a marketplace-oriented business culture only among the bottom end of service workers such as cab drivers and couriers. Still, they provide an interesting sociological test bed for the future, as these marketplace forms of organization begin to replace the current dynamic of employer-to-employee relationships. This phenomenon does not restrict itself to the gig economy. There are plenty of industries that lend themselves to possible 'disruption' by shifting the management of workers in their companies to an algorithm and thereby significantly changing the contract between workers and their employer. IT services is one such example.

Chapter 8

The Modern Business Firm: A Nexus of Contracts

A firm is a nexus of contracts. What that means in simple terms is that a firm or company is a junction point (or nexus) where various contracts come together. These include contracts for purchase of raw materials from suppliers, say, as well as contracts with various other entities or people who help the firm make its product or deliver its service. So, these could be employment contracts, contracts with accountants, lawyers and technology firms, contracts for procurement of direct equipment used on a manufacturing shop floor, furniture, fixtures and so on. Also, and of course, the final sales contract with the customer of the product or service.

The traditional nexus of contracts now runs the risk of being made obsolete in many businesses such as IT and back-office services. I will begin with a small foray into classical economics in an attempt to explain a fundamental change that is about to beset IT and back-office services firms as we know them today. The beauty of any seminal thought in classical economics lies in its ability to engender a reaction in the reader which goes along the lines of, 'Yes, of course, that's true. Everyone knows that.' Everyone may have known it, but it is always the man or woman who first gives voice to the thought who goes on to become a noted economist or win the Nobel Prize!

Ronald Coase, a British–American economist and Nobel laureate, was such a man. About eighty-five years ago, he gave the world a paper called 'The Nature of the Firm' published in the journal *Economica*, in which he posited that the only reason for firms (or companies) to exist was because external economic conditions forced entrepreneurs or owners to employ people and organize them so as to produce goods and services that could be traded in a more cost-effective way than in a free-for-all market. Then prevailing economic conditions meant that the overall costs of thousands of buyers trading with thousands of sellers in order to produce and buy, say, a motor car, was simply too great; the transaction costs themselves would probably far outstrip the cost of the car itself.

So, instead of thousands forming independent relationships for the production and procurement of cars, Henry Ford formed a company, which in turn employed thousands of people in order to produce and sell motor cars to individual buyers. This meant that thousands of car producers (the employees) traded with one entity—Ford Motor Co.—and thousands of buyers also traded with the same company, making Ford a 'nexus of contracts'.

Diagram 3

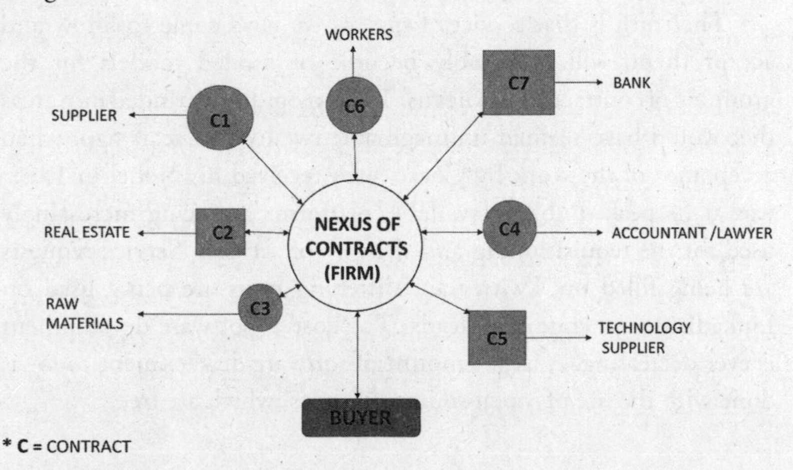

About a half-century later, work on a variation of this theme by William Meckling, Michael 'Mike' Jensen and Kevin Murphy (professors at my alma mater, the University of Rochester) established that there were also intra-company transaction costs called 'agency costs', which arose simply due to the inefficiency of contracts inside each firm. A worker at Ford, who had his or her own personal goals, was not always going to act in the best interest of Henry Ford, the owner.

These economists posited that the best way to get an employee (or agent) to act in the interest of the owner was to compensate the agent in the same way that the owner was compensated. This theory laid the foundation for stock options which soon become an established way for firms to compensate their executives. The impact of this theory was so great that the US Congress changed tax law to make it cost-effective for firms to compensate managers with options. Many a mediocre manager has now a millionaire been made, thanks to Meckling, Mike and Murphy.

Well, prevailing economic conditions have changed, certainly in our neck of the woods. Firms are reneging on employment contracts even before new employees have a chance to start work. Much of this phenomenon has been attributed to 'weak' demand and the rise of automation wherein robots or software do the work of individuals, but these phenomena are only a part of the story.

The truth is that services firms, as we have come to know and accept them, will inexorably become outmoded models for the grouping of contracts into a nexus. Technology has expanded into areas that would have seemed unimaginable twenty-five years ago, when acceptance of the work by Coase, who received his Nobel in 1991, was at its peak. Publicly available platforms are being increasingly used for the requisitioning and delivery of services. Service requests are being filled on Twitter and listening posts are being used on LinkedIn to generate sales leads. The cost of software development is ever decreasing. A large amount of software development today is done with the use of 'open source' libraries, which are free.

In short, the contracting cost around buying and selling software and business services is plummeting. This calls into question whether services firms need to have the same nexus of contracts as they did before or whether the future will be one where services firms increasingly become simply a platform for buyers and sellers to collaborate. The platform will itself only provide a few signature processes that are unique and that all participants in the services market (buyers and sellers) will subscribe to and agree with—and pay for.

In a recent conversation I had with the global head of HR for a large multinational bank, he indicated that he sees only four signature processes that each such platform will need to provide and which it will have to do better than its competition in order to thrive: first, resource allocation (by managing the bidding process for skilled human resources); second, the ability to accurately predict operational risk as an indicator of the potential performance of the worker; third, a feedback mechanism as an ex-post measure of the performance of the worker, and which fourth, over a period of time, will provide an ever-improving database off which to predict the second signature process of operational risk. If his view is accurate, which I think it is, IT and back-office services firms will be turned inside-out over the next decade.

Adding to this is the fact that the COVID-19 outbreak could forever change how people work in the IT world. Every tech business throughout the world, whether a start-up, IT services company or big tech behemoth, is still facing a logistically challenging time.

Silicon Valley's big tech firms were among the first to respond to the crisis of COVID-19 contagion with work-from-home policies. Many prominent technology companies in the US have swiftly moved from recommending that employees work from home to issuing diktats requiring them to do so. There is no doubt that businesses and governments the world over are taking social distancing very seriously. Even an organization like ISIS, which presumes to run an Islamic state, was reported to have issued a warning to its terrorist cadres to 'wash their hands' and run away from people who they thought had the disease, just as they would 'run away from a lion'.

Interestingly, this shift to the gig economy that has held observers agog in recent times was actually born during the world's last big economic crisis of 2008–09, when firms such as Uber, Lyft, Airbnb and other marketplaces were established. COVID-19 might ensure that the hundreds of thousands of full-time employees at IT firms are staring at becoming gig economy contractors very soon.

Large tech firms have not been oblivious to these trends that are reshaping the industry. For instance, Microsoft Inc. has acquired GitHub, a source-code hosting service, and Wipro Ltd. has acquired Top Coder, which is a large platform for dispersed computer programmers to come together to work on specific projects.

To add to this, the social distancing that has now been made a reality by the COVID-19 pandemic will further push the acceptability of remote work, which would create in its wake a 'new normal' from the perspective of actually running an even more aggressively distributed IT operation.

In a two-pronged pincer attack on the world of IT services, another change is afoot. And that is the movement to 'no-code' work when it comes to upgrading technology and platforms. This is already evident in the world of IT where programmers increasingly use open libraries of code written by someone else that they cut and paste into their programs in order to achieve certain functional tasks. This phenomenon is already well known in the IT world and has actually reduced the skill levels at which IT programmers need to perform. Why stress when you can simply drag and drop?

Tangentially, it is also highly likely that AI will end computer programming and testing as we know them today. Our kids needn't acquire skills that advances in machine learning will probably turn obsolete.

During the middle of the pandemic in 2020, an AI lab in San Francisco called OpenAI revealed a technology that has been in the making for some time. This new system, called Generative

Pre-trained Transformer 3 (GPT-3), learnt the nuances of natural language over several months—language as spoken and written by humans. It analysed thousands of digital books and nearly a trillion words posted on the rest of the Internet. GPT-3 is the output of several years of work done by the world's leading AI labs, including OpenAI, which is an independent organization backed by $1 billion in funding from Microsoft.

At Google, a system called Bert (short for Bidirectional Encoder Representations from Transformers) was also trained on a large selection of online words. It can guess missing words in millions of sentences, such as 'I am going to see a man about a....' or 'I am going to... a man about a dog.' These systems are called natural language models and can manage many interfaces, from chatbots and voice commands to Amazon's Alexa or Google. But GPT-3, which learnt language from a far larger set of online text than previous models, opens up many more possibilities.

GPT-3 is what AI scientists call a 'neural network', which is a mathematical system loosely modelled on the web of neurons in the brain. As can be expected of such complexity, there is more than a single mathematical model. The two most widely used are recursive neural networks, which develop a memory pattern, and convolutional neural networks, which develop spatial reasoning. The first is used for tasks such as language translation, and the second for tasks that involve image processing. These neural networks use enormous amounts of computing power, as do other AI neural network models that help with 'deep learning'. Bert and GPT-3 are classified as neural networks that operate on language.

But, unlike Bert, GPT-3 was trained on vastly more data. The first hope was that it could predict the next word in a sentence, rather than just one word anywhere in it, and that it could keep going if you typed a few words—by completing many sentences, and even several paragraphs, based on your original thoughts.

During its long training, GPT-3 parsed out more than 175 billion parameters—mathematical representations of language patterns—

in the vast set of books, Wikipedia articles and other online texts that were in its syllabus for study. These parameters amount to a map of language: i.e., a mathematical description of the way we piece words together.

It can summarize email, generate tweets, write poetry, answer trivia and translate languages. It does all of these with minimal manual help or direction. For many of us who watch developments in AI, GPT-3 represents an unexpected leap towards machines that can understand the ins and outs of language.

For most of today's machine learning or deep learning programs, including image recognition tools for self-driving vehicles, we think of thousands of people in India or Sri Lanka labelling every picture so that an AI program can refer to those labels each time it attempts a task, such as recognizing a traffic sign accurately, or a pedestrian instead of a bicyclist.

Unlike these, GPT-3 can be primed for specific tasks using just a few examples, as opposed to the thousands of examples and several hours of additional training required by its deep learning predecessors. Computer scientists call this 'few-shot learning' and believe that GPT-3 is the first real example of what could be a powerful change in the way humankind trains its machines. It is not just the beginning of a new era for speech recognition programs like Amazon's Alexa or Apple's Siri. The real surprise from GPT-3 is that systems architects have been able to provide just a few simple instructions to let it even write its own computer programs.

At a basic level, computer programs are English-like commands given to a computer in a logical sequence such that the commands produce a certain outcome after a computer acts on them. As such, GPT-3's mathematical descriptions of the way we piece English together works whether we are writing columns or coding software programs. Using these maps, GPT-3 can perform tasks it was not originally built to do.

So far, Open AI has shared GPT-3 with a small number of testers, since many kinks, including biases and profanities, need to be sorted out. That said, Open AI scientists have claimed that 'any layperson can take this model and provide these examples in about five minutes and get useful behaviour out of it'. Unsurprisingly, Microsoft has licensed exclusive use of the source code, but others can use a public interface to generate output.

We are bombarded in India with ads for courses that promise to teach children coding skills. Everyone seems to think that the pandemic has shifted the world firmly towards digitization, and that the only businesses of the future would be technology-enabled ones, or at least those that can quickly pivot themselves to a digital, remote delivery model. Parents seem intent on making their children computer programmers.

It's evident that preying on the gullibility of worried parents is not difficult. But the abilities of GPT-3 demonstrate that we are probably training our children in the skills that will be long obsolete before their work careers are done.

Chapter 9

Late-Industrial-Era Modifications to Business Process Functionality

About seventy years after Taylor's seminal work came the first worthwhile change in management thinking through something called 'Total Quality Management' or TQM. TQM is the continual process of detecting and reducing or eliminating errors in manufacturing, streamlining supply chain management, improving the customer experience and ensuring that employees are up to speed with training. TQM aims to hold all parties involved in the production process accountable for the overall quality of the final product or service.

TQM was developed by William Deming, a management consultant whose work had a great impact on Japanese manufacturing. While TQM shares much in common with the Six Sigma improvement process, it is not the same as Six Sigma. TQM focuses on ensuring that internal guidelines and process standards reduce errors, while Six Sigma looks to reduce defects. Six Sigma is a statistical term used in describing the result of any process. It essentially means that any outlier from a given result occurs less than 99.99966 per cent of times, that is, an infinitesimally small number of times. Let's take the example of manufacturing a car or motorcycle part—say the muffler or silencer in the exhaust system. If a firm manufacturing these mufflers was running its manufacturing and assembly processes at Six Sigma, it would mean that there would be less than 4 mufflers that were defective out of every 1 million produced.

The difference between TQM and Six Sigma is an important one, since the latter can lead to situations where results can be tightly focused on a wrong goal (thereby fulfilling the criteria for Six Sigma but defeating the objective). TQM looks to fix the process, assuming that the result will then take care of itself! As far as I'm concerned, that's almost a metaphysical approach to business!

When I joined Xerox right on the heels of its winning the Malcolm Baldridge Quality Award in 1989, the company had just fought off a massive onslaught from its Japanese competition who were fast gaining share of Xerox's cash cow businesses in photocopying and printing. Xerox's Japanese competitors had become known as forces to reckon with and Japanese manufacturing in the 1980s was considered streets ahead on quality compared to anything made in the US. Their products always worked as they should. This was true from photocopiers to electronic entertainment equipment to motor cars—all areas in which the Japanese had made significant inroads into American market share.

The irony is that TQM was the brainchild of the American Deming, and that Japanese companies were sending entire cohorts of middle managers to America's famed business schools at the time in order to arm themselves with an MBA and come back to work with superior American theory that they could actually put into practice at their firms back home in Japan. I had many Japanese classmates; one who taught me how to eat and enjoy sushi (Ken Yozhisaki, an MBA classmate who introduced me to sushi, promised and swore that he would make sure that I had nothing but cooked food to eat. After I had enjoyed my first sushi meal, and about a half an hour after we had left the restaurant, he smiled and said, 'Who said cooking always involves a fire?').

But I digress. The TQM movement oversees all activities and tasks needed to maintain a desired level of excellence within a business and its operations. This includes the determination of a quality policy, creating and implementing quality planning and assurance, and quality control and quality improvement measures. We were subjected to the quality processes in everything we did at Xerox—including how business meetings were conducted. As a result, we wasted little time—every business activity had predefined quality characteristics, and the company stuck to these like everyone's life depended on it. Quality was certainly a religion at Xerox in the early 1990s and led to a serious rethink on how the company did anything—whether directly associated with manufacturing or not.

Various iterations of TQM have been developed, each with its own set of principles. Still, certain core elements persist. These include putting the customer first, good leadership, a focus on quality, error-correction and improvement as an on-going process, and job training.

The most famous example of TQM is perhaps Toyota's implementation of the Kanban system. A Kanban is a physical signal that creates a chain reaction, resulting in a specific action. Specifically, Toyota used Kanban to implement its just-in-time inventory process. To make its assembly line more efficient, the company decided to keep just enough inventory on hand to fill customer orders as they were generated. Therefore, all parts of Toyota's assembly line are assigned a physical card that has an associated inventory number. Right before a part is installed in a car, the card is removed and moved up the supply chain, effectively requesting another of the same part as a replacement for its spot on the chain. This allows the company to keep its inventory lean and not overstock unnecessary assets. Effective quality management resulted in better automobiles that could be produced at an affordable price.

Some of the quality revolution in America during the 1980s led to the pulling together of all the various forms of thought in TQM into an orthogonal view of the corporation, called the 'Value Chain'. A value chain is a set of activities that a firm operating in a specific industry performs in order to deliver a valuable product and/or service to the market. The concept comes through business management literature and was first described by Michael Porter in his 1985 book *Competitive Advantage: Creating and Sustaining Superior Performance*.

The idea of the value chain is based on the process-driven view of organizations. This entails seeing a manufacturing (or service) organization as a system made up of subsystems, each with inputs, transformation processes and outputs.

Diagram 4

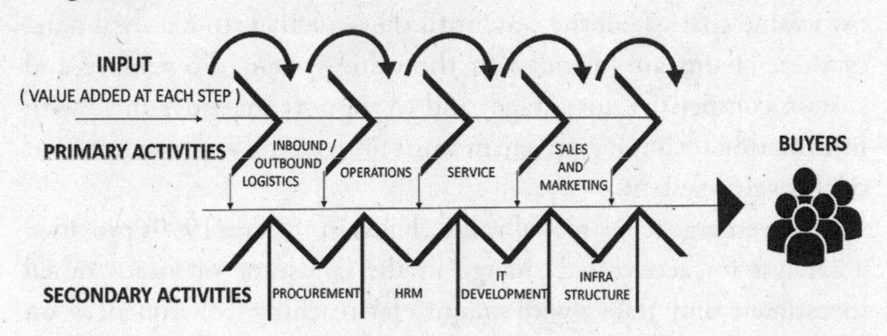

In other words, something enters a business process, is worked upon so that it can be changed, and 'value' added to it, and is then handed off to the next process. The key here is the steps in that business process that add value to what it first received as an input. Inputs, transformation (value add) processes and outputs involve the acquisition and consumption of resources—money, labour, materials, equipment, buildings, land, administration and management. How value chain activities are carried out determines costs and affects profits.

The concept of value chains as decision-support tools was added on to the competitive strategies paradigm developed by Porter and had certainly made its way into business school curricula by the late 1980s, which is when I earned my MBA. In value chain analyses, inbound logistics, operations, outbound logistics, marketing and sales, and service are categorized as primary activities. Secondary activities include procurement, human resource management, technological development and infrastructure.

A firm's value chain forms part of a larger stream of activities, which Porter calls a value 'system'. A value system, or an industry value chain, includes the suppliers that provide the inputs necessary to the firm along with their own subsidiary value chains. After the firm creates products for the market, these products then pass through the value chains of distributors (which also have their own value chains), all the way until they reach customers. All parts of these chains are included in the value system. To achieve and sustain competitive advantage, and to support that advantage with information technologies, a firm must understand every component of this value system.

The emergence of global value chains in the late 1990s provided a catalyst for accelerated change in the landscape of international investment and trade, with major, far-reaching consequences on governments as well as enterprises. Many books on 'globalization' followed, as did the emergence of China as a manufacturing power, where Japan had once held full sway.

The activity of a diamond cutter can illustrate the difference between cost and the value chain. The cutting activity may have a low cost, given that it is largely carried out in low labour cost areas such as Surat in Gujarat, India—but the activity adds much of the value to the end product. A rough diamond is significantly less valuable than a cut diamond. So, the process and its functions, whether direct or supporting, become paramount. In this example, the support processes of logistics and inventory management start the value chain. The uncut stones would have to be economically and efficiently transported to Surat, and distributed to stone cutters first so that they could then perform the core process of cutting the stone. Support processes take over again at that point to have the finished stones shipped out, valued and distributed to selling points all over the world, including famed diamond trading centres in places like Belgium and New York.

Global value chains also extend to support processes such as IT or support business processes, such as invoicing, billing and collections. Miles upon miles of 'dark' fibre were laid underground and undersea during the Internet revolution of the later 1990s. The discovery that work could be more easily moved to the worker than to the work by simply 'lighting up' this fibre so that it would carry data gave rise to India's boom in IT and business process outsourcing in the early 2000s.

Typically, the described value chain and the documentation of processes, assessment and auditing of adherence to the process routines are at the core of the 'quality' certification of the business. In the 1990s, many firms went through large amounts of work to have themselves certified at various levels of quality, such as ISO 9001 and so on. The practice continues until this day.

Primary activities

All five primary activities in the value chain are essential in adding value and creating a competitive advantage. They are:

- **Inbound Logistics:** arranging the inbound movement of materials, parts, and/or finished inventory from suppliers to manufacturing or assembly plants, warehouses or retail stores
- **Operations:** concerned with managing the process that converts inputs (in the forms of raw materials, labour and energy) into outputs (in the form of goods and/or services)
- **Outbound Logistics:** is the process related to the storage and movement of the final product and the related

information flows from the end of the production line to the end user

- **Marketing and Sales:** selling products and processes for creating, communicating, delivering and exchanging offerings that have value for customers, clients, partners and society at large
- **Services:** includes all the activities required to keep the product working effectively for the buyer after it is sold and delivered. You have seen how complicated this function can actually be in my descriptions of Xerox's Field Work Support System earlier in this book.

Support activities

Using support activities helps make primary activities more effective. Increasing any of the four support activities helps at least one primary activity to work more efficiently.

- **Infrastructure:** consists of activities such as accounting, legal, finance, control, public relations, quality assurance and general or strategic management. In many instances, especially in accounting and finance, these have now been automated by the use of software that automatically computes accounts, payments, receivables and so on. Money and its circulation are the lifeblood of any business, and it is not surprising that IT plays a large role here in order to ease the inflows and outflows of money.
- **Technological Development:** pertains to the equipment, hardware, software, procedures and technical knowledge brought to bear in the firm's transformation of inputs (raw materials) into outputs (finished goods). IT has pole position here, quite obviously, as does engineering and technological product development

- **Human Resources:** this consists of all activities involved in recruiting, hiring, training, developing, compensating and (when necessary) dismissing or laying off personnel
- **Procurement:** the acquisition of goods, services or works from an outside external source

A value chain approach could also offer a meaningful alternative to evaluate private or public companies when there is a lack of publicly known data from direct competition, where the subject company is compared with, for example, a known downstream industry to have a good feel of its value by building useful correlations with its downstream companies.

Moreover, it can offer an insight into how e-commerce and m-commerce (mobile commerce) add value in the flow of activities and processes involved in business-to-consumer markets.

Chapter 10

Early-Technology-Era Modifications to Business Process Functionality: 'Transformation' Through Re-engineering and the Dot-Com Boom/Bust Era

After wide acceptance of the value chain as a method for understanding the functional areas of an enterprise, the early 1990s, seventy-five years or so after Taylor's death, saw a new phenomenon. This was the watershed which many of today's largest IT outsourcers used to start their phenomenal growth and at which they became adept over the years. However, the lion's share of the initial 'thought leadership' work was done by top tier consulting firms who then brought in the 'lower' level IT firms to work on the solutions associated with the work they were doing. This phenomenon was the Business Process Re-engineering (BPR) revolution. In my mind, it is a gift that has kept on giving for more than thirty years, not unlike Taylor's Scientific Management, a tool which remained sharp for more than seventy-five years.

BPR began as a private sector technique to help organizations rethink how they do their work in order to improve customer service, cut operational costs and become world-class competitors. A key stimulus for re-engineering has been the continuing development and deployment of information systems and networks. Organizations are becoming bolder in using this technology to support business processes, rather than refining current ways of doing work.

In 1990, Michael Hammer, a former professor of computer science at the Massachusetts Institute of Technology (MIT), published the article 'Reengineering Work: Don't Automate, Obliterate' in *Harvard Business Review*, in which he claimed that the major challenge for managers is to obliterate forms of work that do not add value, rather than using technology for automating it. This statement implicitly accused managers of having focused on the wrong issues, namely that technology in general, and more specifically information technology, has been used primarily for automating existing processes rather than using it as an enabler for making non-value adding work obsolete.

Hammer's claim was simple. According to him, most of the work being done does not add any value for customers, and this work should be removed, not accelerated through automation or through the use of technology. Instead, companies should reconsider their inability to satisfy customer needs, and their insufficient cost structures. Even well-established management thinkers, such as Peter Drucker (who had long venerated Frederick Taylor) and Tom Peters, were accepting and advocating BPR as a new tool for achieving success in a dynamic world. During the following years, a fast-growing number of publications, books as well as journal articles, were dedicated to BPR and many consulting firms embarked on this trend and developed BPR methods. However, the critics were quick to claim that BPR was a way to dehumanize the workplace, increase managerial control, and justify downsizing. Despite this critique, re-engineering was adopted at an accelerating pace and by the early nineties, the majority of Fortune 500 companies claimed to either have initiated re-engineering efforts, or had plans to do so.

BPR is the practice of rethinking and redesigning the way work is done to better support an organization's mission and reduce costs. The entire theory is that businesses had built themselves in a reactive mode as time had gone by and, as a result, had become inefficient due to a variety of extra processes and systems that may have been put in place to address ad hoc needs. As a result, according to BPR theorists, firms were an agglomeration of unnecessary processes, systems, and yes, unnecessary people.

Re-engineering starts with a high-level assessment of the organization's mission, strategic goals, and customer needs. Basic (and largely woolly and unanswerable) questions were asked, such as, 'Does our mission need to be redefined?', 'Are our strategic goals aligned with our mission?', 'Who are our customers?' According to BPR champions, an organization would very likely find that it was operating on questionable assumptions, particularly in terms of the wants and needs of its customers. In the mind of these practitioners, only after the organization rethinks what it should be doing, does it go on to decide how best to do it.

BPR theorists and practitioners tried to help organizations re-engineer two key areas of their businesses. First, they used (then) modern technology to enhance data dissemination and decision-making processes. These would include things such as management dashboards, drill-down reports and a variety of ways to provide data into what were called 'decision support systems'.

Within the framework of this basic assessment of mission and goals, re-engineering focused on the organization's business processes—the steps and procedures that govern how resources are used to create products and services that meet the needs of particular customers or markets. Conceptually, as a structured ordering of work steps across time and place, a business process can be decomposed into specific activities, measured, modeled and improved. BPR practitioners held that these processes could also be completely redesigned or eliminated altogether. Re-engineering identified, analysed and redesigned an organization's core business processes with the aim of achieving improvements in critical performance measures, such as cost, quality, service and speed.

Re-engineering assumed that an organization's business processes are usually fragmented into sub-processes and tasks that are carried out by several specialized functional areas within the organization. However, often no one was responsible for the overall performance of the entire process. Re-engineering maintained that optimizing the performance of sub-processes could result in some benefits but could not yield improvements if the process itself was fundamentally inefficient and not in keeping with modern changes. For that reason, re-engineering focused on redesigning the process as a whole to achieve the greatest possible benefits to the organization and their customers. This drive for realizing improvements by fundamentally rethinking how the organization's work should be done distinguished re-engineering from earlier TQM process improvement efforts that focused on functional or incremental improvement.

Despite Hammer's original bold assertions that IT could be minimized by adopting BPR, the BPR wave actually spawned a boom in the adoption of new technology that vendors claimed had been 're-engineered' to fit old business processes. Companies such as SAP and Oracle—in many ways almost household names today—staked their business in coming up with 'Enterprise Resource Planning' or ERP software products that were behemoths in their design and scope. Entire corporations ditched their old COBOL/CICS systems (such as Xerox's Field Work Support System that I described in the third chapter) for newer versions of software that performed the same business functions, but supposedly in re-engineered (and therefore supposedly more cost-competitive) manner.

Firms such as Oracle, Baan, SAP and others redesigned a bunch of work processes from scratch and created highly templatized pieces of software capable of performing business processes with great precision. These, however, took much effort to customize and integrate with existing IT systems at clients. While the top tier consulting firms were capable of providing the business process specifics as well as the oversight, they had, at the time, not yet staffed themselves up to the point where the 'dirt under the fingernails' work of bolting on large unwieldy ERP systems could be done in-house. This led corporations in the US, the UK, Australia and several other countries to allow the still nascent Indian software integration firms such as Infosys, Wipro, TCS and others to grow in the wake of the white shoe consultants' recommended changes.

Meanwhile, the dot-com bubble of the late 1990s and early 2000s was a speculative economic bubble created by excessive optimism towards Internet companies and their shares. The 1990s were a period of rapid technological advancement. Mosaic, the world's first Internet browser was created in 1993 and allowed individuals to access the World Wide Web from their personal computers. Soon after, personal computers slowly changed from being a luxury product to becoming essential in many homes in the US. There was a mass adoption of Internet usage and entrepreneurs began to see untapped potential within this industry. The result was an enormous wave of new Internet companies, such as Amazon and Yahoo, among thousands of others.

One of the most influential enterprises during this period was Netscape Communications. In 1995, Netscape released and distributed its own Internet browser called the Netscape Navigator—for free. With a faster and more intuitive user interface, it quickly overtook Mosaic as the most popular web browser. Navigator soon became the new industry standard. Despite this success, Netscape still had no steady streams of revenue and was operating with losses. And in a reprise oft seen in today's brave new technology world, despite the losses, the founders of Netscape decided to take advantage of the browser's success and took the company public.

On 9 August of the same year, Netscape had their Initial Public Offering (IPO), taking the world by storm. Investors generally make investments based on a company's past performance and its profit margins. But with the Internet's exponential growth and the success of Navigator, they found this opportunity too hard to pass up. The stock was listed at $28 on its first morning of active trading and soared to $58.25 on the same day, pushing the company's market capitalization to upwards of $2.5 billion in what was until then probably the most successful IPO of all time. I remember that week clearly. I bought some shares of Netscape before leaving on a biking trip with friends to the Bridger-Teton and Yellowstone National Parks. All we could speak of was the Netscape IPO.

Around the mid-1990s, interest rates in the US had fallen to significant lows and capital gains taxes had been reduced tremendously. Because of this, investors now had more capital, which allowed them to make more speculative investments in dot-com companies. Low interest rates made borrowing less expensive for entrepreneurs who needed loans to start their new Internet ventures. This resulted in a large number of new Internet companies being formed. The success of Netscape's IPO inspired this new wave of entrepreneurs and investors to take their companies public, and venture capital investors rushed to fund them.

While the dot-com bubble was underway in the US, India was witnessing a different kind of revolution: fighting the Y2K bug. Existing global computer systems at the time had been designed to signify the year with two digits (instead of four) to save memory space. The systems which were at risk (and no one knew exactly which systems had this bug), could end up in a completely unpredictable state at the turn of the century. Companies were racing against time to reprogram their systems—in other words, fix the bug—before the dreaded midnight hour rang in the new millennium.

Going through millions of lines of computer code was a massive task for the existing workforce, and companies in the US started outsourcing large chunks of this work to IT services. This, in turn, led to a boom in the Indian IT services sector and is believed to have been crucial in helping India become an IT hotspot. Interestingly, many US IT services companies did not staff up significantly to meet the Y2K challenge. I was working for IBM at the time, the company that was arguably the main cause of the Y2K bug, since it was IBM programmers and computer scientists that had neglected to code in four digits to represent a year in computer systems, and had only coded in two. Even so, IBM did not create a large Y2K practice. The work was considered short-term, and almost scavenger-like. The joke among IBMers and other US-headquartered IT services firms was that all the Indian programmers who had newly shown up on American shores was that these programmers would soon be B2B (as in going 'Back to Bangalore').

From 1995 to 1999, hundreds of dot-com companies had their IPOs and received immediate responses from the public and retail investors. However, one theme united the majority of these companies. They spent hundreds of millions of dollars on marketing to expand their market share and user base (called 'eyeballs' at the time). With sales growth being one of the only factors that investors looked at, most companies began to employ growth-at-any-cost tactics. Some even sold products at a loss and made acquisitions to maintain their market share. Many companies squandered large sums of money.

As a result of all this spending on growing their user bases, profits at these companies were practically non-existent. At the time, however, this appeared not to matter because their ultimate goal was to get as many users to utilize their Internet-based products. In 1999 alone, 486 companies had their IPOs, most of which were dot-com stocks. Of these 300 dot-com stocks, 117 of them had their stocks double in value on the first day of trading.

In the rush to cash in on the Internet boom, many investors ignored traditional investment metrics, such as the ratio of a company's current share price compared to its per-share earnings (P/E ratio). Instead, they subscribed to a business model that favoured building brand awareness and market share quickly, even if that required offering services or products for free. These factors, combined with the seemingly overnight fortunes made by some of the start-up founders whose companies went public, fueled the greed.

As Paul Volcker, then chairman of America's Federal Reserve (akin to India's Reserve Bank of India) famously said investors' 'irrational exuberance' was causing stocks to be bid up instead of any fundamental analysis of the profit performance of the businesses themselves.

One or two of the businesses created during those heady times survive to this day. Most, however, crashed and burnt, but in today's new age of a plethora of data caused by Internet usage, firms with the same business models from twenty-five years ago have seen a resurrection as artificial intelligence and machine learning companies. Innovations like home delivery of groceries and meats are not recent. George Sheehan, the worldwide boss of Accenture, was lured away by the possibility of making billions in a short time by heading off to create WebVan, a company based on making purchases at grocery stores and then delivering the groceries in exact size lots to match what consumers ordered from the comfort of their homes. My boss at IBM, Stephen Mucchetti, who was then a peer to Ginni Rommetty (later IBM's CEO), went off to a senior position at Scient, an early Internet consulting firm. Mucchetti had earlier been the global boss of Coopers & Lybrand and was a highly respected business executive. Scient, like most firms of that era, finally crashed and burnt in the dot-com bust of 2000–01. If you think I am sounding a warning here about what is currently happening in stock markets around the world, where fundamentals have been replaced by speculative frenzy, you are right.

The Indian IT services firms, while becoming behemoths themselves in the aftermath of both the ERP systems that were made to support BPR efforts, as well as the Y2K phenomenon, made an error. This would relegate Indian firms and the computer programmers who worked for them to become followers rather than leaders as far as innovation and high-level design work was concerned. The error was simple—to increase the quality of the code they wrote, and in response to the sheer volume of work coming in, these firms transformed themselves into a 'factory' model. This allowed them to win coveted 'Software Development Quality' certifications, such as the almost unattainable Level 5 of the Software and Capability and Maturity Model (CMM). Indian programmers went from being criticized for the quality of their work to becoming role models for software development quality in less than five years. When I returned to India in 2002, over sixty of the seventy or so sites all over the world that had been certified as CMM Level 5 were in one city: Bangalore.

To achieve these certifications, the work that Indian software services firms did was parcelled out in ever smaller pieces to the point that no one programmer really could understand how his or her work fit into the whole picture. Larger non-Indian companies, both competitors of the Indian IT services firms as well as their own clients, such as JP Morgan, Goldman Sachs and countless others, followed suit by setting up 'captive' centres to which disjointed pieces of technology work were parsed out and sent. This is the kind of computer programmer that such IT services hire in droves: people who can write code for ever smaller slivers of work. All the while, they have no idea how the computer code they're writing affects anything for the enterprise.

Don't become one of them. Instead, within your business or for your employer, figure out what role you can play to make the most of ongoing technological change, and play that role.

Section III

Chapter 11

Playing Your Roles Well—Understanding Who You Really Are

Before we start talking in earnest about the roles you can play within your organization as technology changes our world, I will borrow heavily upon modern 'self-help' or 'spiritual' readings from authors such as Eckhart Tolle and Michael Singer to dwell upon an important aspect of our personalities and psychologies.

I need to let you in on a secret. I talk to myself. No, not out loud! In my head. The tone of the voice talking is usually borrowed from whatever emotion I am feeling at the time. If it is fear, the voice whines in a cacophony of all sorts of catastrophic endings. In the absence of knowledge, it looks for the worst possible outcomes in a given scenario, and then plays out each horrific scene in lurid detail. If I am going through a particularly stressful time, it speaks as I try to lull myself to sleep at night, and, as soon as I wake up in the morning, it starts up again.

Every once in a while, there are multiple voices with different personalities. My mind retorts to its own whining from a moment earlier with the rejoinder: 'You're crazy, there's no way that could happen. Calm down and take it easy.' If the sponsoring emotion emanates from a recent success, it crows and fawns. It says there is no one who is its equal. And there too, it sometimes splits personality mid-stream. It says: 'You were just lucky, stop beating your own drum.'

Had I made a public admission about talking to myself with these voices in my head a few years ago, while sitting on the board of a company where I was one of the seniormost executives, I am sure that I would have been met with looks of horror. I may even have been told to find a good therapist—and fast. You see, no one likes to admit to themselves, much less to others, that they have voices in their heads. We are brought up in cultures where we are taught not to show our vulnerable insides to anyone else. Looking for help with mental health professionals can often be construed as a sign of weakness. Even in countries like the US, where mental health is taken seriously, no one openly admits at work that they need or are seeking help. These situations are kept totally out of the workplace.

I'm not alone. The truth is that all of us have these voices. Let me demonstrate with a simple example. Sometimes, we have to ask a person whom we are conversing with to repeat themselves because our minds had 'wandered' and we hadn't heard what they said. Well, what was our mind doing when it wandered? Talking, of course.

For some of us, these voices are too much to bear. We turn to legal (and sometimes illegal) ways of medicating ourselves. Across most of the world, the legal drug of choice is alcohol. In some areas, the use of marijuana has been legalized. The US is in the middle of a huge crisis, caused by the misuse of prescription opioid medication. This skirts legality somewhat, since if you can just get a doctor to prescribe it for you, your use is 'legal'. Just like alcohol, these drugs promise escape from our reality and, most important, from that voice in the head. Even if the voice in the head doesn't drop off completely, these drugs certainly help the voice change its tone. The underlying emotion fleetingly provided to the voice is either exhilaration or numbness. Both states of mind work. Temporarily. The next morning, the voice returns again, this time louder, and in its original tone. In binge and habitual users, all the voice wants is to get its next fix.

But what of the voice? Is it me? If so, which voice is me? The whiner? Or the one that tells it to stop whining? Or both? What I have come to realize but can't always remember is that the voices are not me. *This realization is the Master Key*. Instead, who I really am is the listener. Put another way, I am the audience, not the actors. Once I consciously turn my attention to who I really am, I have automatically created the space and ability to see and better understand the battle of the voices in my head.

This happens especially when we are met with a fear of the unknown. As humans, we need certainty, even if it is dire, just so we can prepare ourselves. In its absence, we at least need some predictability. Hence the pundits present themselves in times of trouble and make predictions about what might happen in the future, and we hang on to their every word, just so that we can model what our future might look like.

The simple understanding that the voices are not us takes away the power of the mind and its voices. But arriving at the point where one can take this step, and thereafter stay at that level of conscious thinking, does not come easy. For most, it takes discernment to understand the battle and the will to overcome the voices. Some secular and almost all spiritual texts the world over provide us with plenty of instruction on how to get there through the process of meditation, prayer and self-reflection.

That would mean that the first smart technique to adopt when turbulent change occurs is for us to sit back and realize that we are only witnesses to both our internal emotions as well as the ongoing external change taking place. This allows us to intentionally *respond* to the change rather than unthinkingly *react* to it.

Sometimes, life is much like watching a movie unfold on the screen; some of us laugh at the funny bits and cry at the sad bits, while others don't because they know that the movie they are seeing is unreal. It is so too in real life: what actually occurs to us depends upon us as observers, and not so much on what is observed.

When we create enough space to be witnesses to ourselves, we are free to choose our responses, and therefore alter the reality we experience. This is the second technique. And only human beings can do this, not automatons or computers or robots as they are soulless beings, bereft of sentience, and as a result, can never be a witness to their own machinations. They can only react in the manner their set of computer instructions tells them to. They can never respond. We, however, can choose to respond instead of reacting.

How, then, do we respond?

Do we respond from the same autonomic plane of 'fight or flight' that the more primitive parts of our brains are said to be hardwired for? If so, we have lost the ability to be witnesses to ourselves and therefore also the means to respond intentionally instead of reacting in fear. No, it is by developing some sort of personal peace pact with the 'harmony' or 'disharmony' that is larger than us, and then by going about using our free will in accordance with that harmony; not in opposition to it. This book is an attempt to inform you enough about the changes in technology so that you can develop that personal peace pact, and intentionally respond to the changes around you.

If we fight reality, like many of us might want to, and react instead of responding, we will only get regret, stress and worry. Hence, the truth, best expressed by Viktor Frankl (1905–97), who said in his book *Man's Search for Ultimate Meaning*: 'The last of the human freedoms: to choose one's attitude in any given set of circumstances, to choose one's own way. And there were always choices to make. Every day, every hour, offered the opportunity to make a decision, a decision which determined whether you would or would not submit to those powers which threatened to rob you of your very self, your inner freedom; which determined whether or not you become the plaything to circumstance, renouncing freedom and dignity . . .'

Or more simply put: 'We get to choose how we respond. It is the one freedom that no one can confiscate.'

Chapter 12

Musings for the Soldier

The increasing demand and necessity for certain career fields in the market does not always equate to expectations meeting reality. Any new kind of system must first be built and that requires 'grunt' work, as is happening currently in the field of data science.

Big data or data science is now one of the hottest fields in the market. It consists, supposedly, of any discipline that can combine the fields of statistics and computer science.

Statistics provide data for behavioural (and other) prediction models or algorithms. Algorithms form the underpinning of AI and are linked with statistical concepts that have been around for aeons. Old-style statistical regression modelling and Box-Jenkins time series analyses look for causality and correlations in data and can predict outcomes over periods of time. The computer science side of big data allows for programmers to convert paper algorithms into computer code that can compute the result.

The huge availability of computing power today means that these predictions and behavioural associations can be made in fractions of a second. This allows your web search provider or social networking site to serve advertisements just nanoseconds after you have shown interest in a product. And since everything you do online is supposedly stored on a server somewhere forever, all your past online forays can be instantly called up by an algorithm to predict the next thing you are going to want to do.

Many people who move into the field of data science are able to do so without formal training at traditional institutes of higher learning. This is because demand for employees who possess these skills has grown much more rapidly than what traditional academic institutions have been able to meet. It seems that anyone with a passing familiarity with mathematics or statistics as well as the ability to write programs can easily pole-vault himself or herself into a high-paying career.

Big data seems to fall in the same realm as many other tech buzzwords. No one quite knows what it is. Dan Ariely, a professor of psychology and behavioural economics at Duke University, in a cutting assessment of the field, says, 'Big data is like teenage sex: everyone talks about it, nobody really knows how to do it, everyone thinks everyone else is doing it, so everyone claims they are doing it.'

In a world where the very definition of a field is fuzzy and many employees as well as employers are upstarts, there is a vast mismatch between expectations and reality. The data scientist walks into a job with high expectations of sitting at a desk and working out complex algorithms, while the reality is that most employers are at ground zero—where they need to find data which is stored in silos within their own organizations and convert this into a centralized repository which can be accessed by various computer systems. This means that most 'data scientists' find themselves as little more than resources in an effort to categorize and pool data, or to run queries on data in existing silos, which are all boring tasks.

It looks as though the field of data science is back to the days of the IT outsourcing boom, when employee attrition and job-hopping were the operating realities that every firm in the sector had to live with.

* * *

The implications of new tech can be profound and far-reaching. But in order to adapt to such changes, one must first understand the depth of change that any new technology can affect. Consider the rise of 'bots'.

Automation Anywhere, and its competitors such as UiPath and Blue Prism, are in the business of creating bots, or discrete pieces of software that can automate a lot of work carried out by office workers today.

The first targets of these bot makers are jobs that do not have great complexity. Think of an accounts payable clerk in your office, for instance. All he or she does today is complete a two-way or a three-way match of the amount payable against an invoice—with an existing purchase order—or with both the purchase order as well as another document, such as one that records the receipt of goods specified on the invoice, before approving the invoice and initiating payment.

The worker is usually using computer systems such as ERP systems that automated the paperwork associated with such transactions in a previous wave of automation that took place a couple of decades ago. At that time, it was systems from Germany's SAP or the US' Oracle that automated these paper-driven processes to create the sub-class of Information Technology Enabled Services or ITeS. Indian outsourcing firms had a fair share both in the implementation and the ITeS administration of such ERP systems.

The first step in setting up a bot is to create a 'recorder' that cohabits a worker's computer. It then learns the basics of the job over a few days, by recording keystrokes as the worker does his or her job, noting which parts of ERP systems are accessed by the worker and in what sequence to complete a series of tasks. In a short while, the recorder learns a large proportion of the repetitive tasks a worker performs.

After the recording has been completed, a team of computer programmers converts the recorded actions into an automated script that can run on demand. Interestingly, the amount of programming required to create a bot is quite minimal. Since the bot can now totally replicate what the human has so far been doing, it simply replaces the human.

This is not the job loss we fear from AI. It is the replacing of manual processes with mechanized ones, much as a tractor replaces the need for multiple farm hands. This last bit of office automation by bots is just the icing on a cake that was baked twenty years ago.

This next step of automation was always inevitable. It would have actually taken place in the early 2000s if the Indian offshoring industry had not risen. All that the rise of Indian IT and ITeS offshoring did was to provide a mezzanine step, since it was cheaper to export the repetitive work to destinations like India or the Philippines than it was to automate them. A mezzanine landing is not meant to be occupied for a long time; traffic must inevitably make its way upward—or downward—on the staircase.

Predictions about the job loss due to new technologies are imprecise, largely because bot-led automation is already here, while AI growth is on a trajectory that is difficult for most experts to predict. The one prediction that seemed most balanced was from a report called 'Jobs Lost, Jobs Gained' by the McKinsey Global Institute. The report includes many of the 'it depends' type of answers that is the wont of consultants—but is nonetheless a fine piece of work. Its prediction? India will lose 56.9 million jobs—or 'full-time equivalents'—by 2030.

* * *

The ability to spot inefficiencies in any system is a valuable skill. The ability to do this before any real 'damage' is caused is even more important. Often times, only major events or incidents reveal the fragility of certain systems. For example, the COVID-19 pandemic is what laid bare some of the problems currently plaguing the realm of machine learning.

As a concept, ML represents the idea that a computer, when fed with enough raw data, can begin on its own to see patterns and rules in these numbers. It can also learn to recognize, categorize and feed new data upon arrival into the patterns and rules already created by the computer program. As more data is received, it adds to the 'intelligence' of the computer by making its patterns and rules ever more refined and reliable.

There is still a small but pertinent inconvenience that deserves our attention. Despite the great advances in computing, it is still very difficult to teach computers both human context and basic common sense. The brute-force approach of GPT-3 and Bert that I have discussed earlier in this book, and which is powering AI behemoths does not rely on well-codified rules based on common sense. It relies instead on the raw computing power of machines to sift thousands upon thousands of potential combinations before selecting the best answer using pattern-matching. This applies as much to questions that are intuitively answered by five-year-olds as it does to a medical image diagnosis.

These same algorithms have been guiding decisions made by businesses for a while now—especially strategic and other shifts in corporate direction based on consumer behaviour. In a world where corporations make binary choices (either path X or path Y, but not both), these algorithms still fall short.

The pandemic has exposed their insufficiency further. This is especially true with ML systems at e-commerce retailers that were initially programmed to make sense of our online behaviour. During the pandemic, our online behaviour has been volatile. News reports in various Western countries that kept e-commerce alive during their lockdowns have focused on retailers trying to optimize toilet paper stocks one week and stay-at-home board games the next.

The disruption in ML is widespread. Our online buying behaviour influences a whole hoard of subsidiary computer systems. These are in areas such as inventory and supply chain management, marketing, pricing, fraud detection and so on.

To an interested observer, it would appear that many of these algorithms base themselves on stationary assumptions about data. Detailed explanations of how stationary processes are used for statistical data modelling and predictions can be found online if you're interested in understanding the statistics and mathematics behind this assumption about data. Very simply put, however, this means that algorithms assume that the rules haven't changed—or won't change due to some event in the future. Surprisingly, this goes against the basic admonition that almost all professional investors bake into their fine print, especially the one that says, 'Past performance is no predictor of future performance.'

The paradox is that finding patterns and then using them to make useful predictions is what ML is all about in the first place. But static assumptions have meant that the data sets used to train ML models haven't included anything more than elementary 'worst case' information. They didn't expect a pandemic.

Also, bias, even when it is not informed by such negative qualities as racism, is often added into these algorithms long before they spit out computer code. The bias enters through the way an ML solution is framed, the presence of 'unknown unknowns' in data sets, and in how the data is prepared before it is fed into a computer. For instance, the relative inability of facial recognition technology to accurately identify darker-skinned faces has been linked to multiple wrongful arrests of black men, an issue stemming from imbalanced data sets, and not from bias added by programmers. Also by the very nature of ML-enabled systems, algorithms may change, or respond to input or output in ways that cannot be anticipated or easily reproduced for forensic analysis.

Compounding such biases is the phenomenon of an 'echo chamber' that is created by finely targeted algorithms that these companies use. The original algorithms induced users to stay online longer and bombarded them with an echo-chamber overload of information that served to reinforce what the algorithm thinks the searcher needs to know. For instance, if I search for a particular type of phone on an e-commerce site, future searches are likely to auto-complete with that phone showing up even before I key in my entire search string. The algorithm gets thrown off when I search for toilet paper instead.

The situation brought about by the COVID-19 pandemic is still volatile and fluid. The training data sets and the computer code they produce to adjust predictive ML algorithms are unequal to the volatility. They need constant manual supervision and tweaking so that they do not throw themselves and other sophisticated downstream automated processes out of gear. It appears that consistent human involvement in automated systems will be around for quite some time.

Inefficiencies can be hidden by the promise of potential in new technologies. It is nevertheless important to be able to identify the setbacks and problems currently plaguing a potential new technology. One can look at how AI reveals that computers are bad at 'learning'.

AI is deeply linked with ML. In fact, almost all of AI today is simply ML—in other words, an attempt to get a computer to make itself more efficient at its task without the need for human intervention. As an investor in deep tech and science companies, I have had the occasion to see several start-ups that claim to use AI/ML.

Neither AI nor ML are deep tech. The applicability of ML is limited, at least today, primarily to the field of data science, where one is actually only trying to ask simple questions of a data set. Most of these questions revolve around whether there is a pattern to the data that is present in the data set, and seek to answer fairly simple questions, such as, 'Is this customer likely to buy product X if they have already bought product Y?' or 'Does this medical scan contain evidence of cancer?'

ML tries to filter out the 'noise' from a data set and arrive at a 'signal'. This is the realm of 'data science'. Data science draws on inductive reasoning—as opposed to the deductive reasoning of arithmetic and algebra. While the conclusion of a deductive process is certain, the truth of the end of an inductive reasoning process is only probable. Statistical modelling allows an ML program to systematically quantify and reason about the inherent uncertainties of inductive reasoning. Every set of data being thrown at an ML model is confusing, especially when the data contained in it is at a large scale.

The confusion in these large data sets will mean that there are four possible outcomes while looking for a signal: a) that the actual data point represents a true positive (as in, yes, this scan shows cancer); b) that the data point represents a true negative (as in there is no cancer); c) a false positive (as in, yes, this scan indicates cancer, when in fact cancer doesn't exist); and d) a false negative (as in, no, this scan doesn't indicate cancer, when in fact cancer is present).

One very soon begins to see that the test data used to 'teach' a machine to 'learn' on its own becomes crucial. This is why many start-ups promise to generate new data sets that can later be used to train an ML model. This 'data exhaust' is presumed to be useful simply because it produces voluminous new data about a subject. Just because one can use ML, it doesn't necessarily follow that the ML model is useful. Neither does it follow that a particular ML model is more effective than a different ML model.

The good news is that there are plenty of ways to gauge the effectiveness of an ML model, but they can be brought down to the four types of predictions I described above (positives, negatives, false positives and false negatives).

The first of these is the prevalence of positives in the data set being used to train the model, and the accuracy of the model in picking those positives.

Let us say only 10 per cent of 1 lakh medical scans that the ML model is being fed to learn from actually indicate the presence of cancer. This number is important, since it gives us a base measure of what the ML model should be able to achieve on its own, after it has worked its way through the vast maze of positives, negatives, false positives and false negatives.

In a random pick from this data set, the probability that the pick is positive is 10 per cent and 90 per cent that it is negative. The start-up's ML model should be much more accurate than a random pick. However, the issue with this strict statistical measure of 'accuracy' is that it includes both positives and negatives (the ML model should be accurate at predicting both).

This can present a problem, since the model could easily pick all negatives (which constitute 90 per cent of the data set in this instance) and still be 100 per cent accurate. However, it would be useless, since this 'accurate' model hasn't been able to pick any of the cancer-positive scans.

The second is the ML model's precision. Precision is the number of true positives that the model finds. The start-up's ML model precision would have to be significantly greater than the prevalence of true positives (10 per cent) in the example. Otherwise, the model is only as good as any random choice at predicting an outcome.

Now, let's assume the model's precision is 100 per cent. The next measure will be its ability to collect true positives from the data set. So, in a data set with 1 lakh medical scans, with 10,000 instances of cancer (10 per cent), the efficacy of the model's collection depends on how many instances of cancer it detects.

Although its precision is now 100 per cent, if it only detects 5000 out of the 10,000 true instances, its collection rate means it has missed the other 5000. These two measures are trade-offs between one another. Decreasing the model's precision can increase its collection, but now in addition to more than 5000 true cases, it will also collect noise: negatives, false negatives and false positives.

There are various other complexities when models deal with sensitive data. Predicting a repeat buy of a pair of jeans is very different from detecting cancer. Despite large data exhausts, sane professionals who understand the field need to come in and help train the model. We will need expert humans for a while yet.

* * *

Another thing to consider with technology is the issue of security with regard to data privacy. In late 2018, reports filtered through that Google would shut down Google+, the company's social networking answer to Facebook, by August 2019, though corporate versions that had been set up solely for use within a corporation might still exist.

This was after Google announced that data from up to 5 lakh users may have been exposed to external developers by a bug that was present for more than two years in its systems. Google said that it had become aware of this breach and patched the leak in March of that year. The tech titan chose not to make this breach public then, and waited six months before it finally made the information public. According to news reports, the company came clean only after it became aware that the *Wall Street Journal* was planning to write an exposé about the breach.

Other news the same week revealed that Facebook's systems had also been breached, with up to 30 million accounts potentially compromised. Facebook was a little more forthcoming about its problems and revealed the issue soon after it became aware of it. Facebook first feared that about 50 million users' personal data had been compromised, including—evidently—chief executive officer Mark Zuckerberg's private information. This number was later reported as being higher, and the company automatically logged out 90 million users from their accounts as a precautionary measure.

This breach was of users' 'access tokens', which is a code that identifies the user and allows other apps to access user information. Many people use their Google or Facebook accounts as gateways to the Internet. When a user signs on to a new app, he or she is often allowed to sign in just by using his or her Facebook or Google access token credentials, which obviates the need to set up a separate account and password for the new app. This is a convenient option for many, and so is routinely used for any number of e-commerce and other sites.

Facebook later said that the number of people affected may be 30 million rather than 50 million, but the data that was compromised was much more detailed. Its fears were that up to 14 million of the 30 million had detailed information compromised, such as their religious affiliations, email addresses and the types of computing devices they used to reach Facebook—in addition to more mundane information such as recent posts and locations. Facebook claimed that credit card data and passwords were not stolen.

Under the new General Data Protection Regulations (GDPR), alerting regulators in Europe within seventy-two hours of discovering a breach is now law. The alarming regularity with which such breaches seem to happen is of great concern. In my mind, more countries need to follow Europe's example in order to make sure their citizens' data is safe.

US federal law, for instance, does not require that companies disclose security vulnerabilities. This law appears to be a state subject in the US and, so, companies must instead work through varying legislations across US states, of which California's seems the most stringent.

Working for the good of the organization also involves understanding the variety of ways in which certain issues can be handled. Take, for example, the issue of information security. Governments, corporations and individuals the world over now worry about information security and the possibility that their computers and data can be compromised. In addition, they are getting very protective of their citizens' rights regarding the use of personal data. The introduction of Europe's GDPR laws around data privacy and security has again brought this issue front and centre, and many firms are scrambling to prove that they comply. India is now preparing its own laws and guidelines around data privacy and it is likely that the proposed Personal Data Protection Bill (PDPB) will also focus on specific limitations on what data can be collected, requirements for prior consent, and on establishing a regulatory body to protect and regulate citizens' personal data.

Late in 2018, I met with Neil Daswani, an expert in information security. We discussed the role of a chief information security officer (CISO) in today's organizations.

He maintains that the organization's own attitude to security is what determines the effectiveness of the CISO. He pointed me to a paper written by Gary McGraw and others from Synopsys, a firm that specializes in security solutions and in ensuring the integrity of its clients' software. The paper categorizes organizations into four distinct CISO 'tribes'.

The lowest grouping is the 'cost centre' tribe, which is overwhelmed and under-resourced. In most cases, security leadership exists deep in the organization, at levels well below executive leadership and middle management. The upper layers of management treat security as a cost centre. In today's world, this tribe is the most exposed.

The second is the 'compliance' tribe. The authors maintain that compliance with regulations such as GDPR is both a boon and bane for security, and that this tribe intentionally leverages compliance requirements to make real security progress. In many cases, previous security leadership in this tribe was replaced at the same time that a compliance regime was imposed from the outside, sometimes in the wake of a crisis. According to McGraw et al., many of these firms still continue to underinvest in security. They maintain that in such companies, though the compliance spending of today may now be more than the pre-crisis spending of yesterday, it is still inadequate to meet future crises. Further, compliance alone does not keep hackers with malicious intent out.

CISOs in the 'compliance' tribe tend not to be deep technologists but, according to McGraw and clan, do tend to have strong managerial and leadership skills. This can lead to a situation in which these CISOs' limited resources are correctly allocated and clear progress is made. However, the organization's overall progress is still inadequate because it is always in 'catch-up' mode after a crisis, or after external regulations such as GDPR have been imposed.

The third is the 'technology' tribe. Its approach to security is not bounded by compliance alone. However, the CISO is likely to have come from a purely technology-based background and tends to overemphasize the definition of security problems in terms of technical aspects alone. According to McGraw and his co-authors, an undersupply of business acumen leads to what they call the 'superman syndrome', in which the 'technology CISO' often gets down in the weeds on particular problems instead of delegating, and learns about the business impacts only through trial and error.

The top grouping is described by McGraw and his collaborators as the 'enabler' tribe. Firms that fit this definition have evolved their security mission to an organization-wide commitment, rather than a simple compliance measure. Security for them is not just a technical problem; it is a business issue. This means that various lines of business actively participate in the overall firm's security mission. CISOs in such firms are on par with senior executives, who lead other business lines. They are proactive and get in front of security issues, both internally and externally, and can intentionally influence the standards by which they will be judged.

* * *

Detecting threats also involves identifying where value can be added to a system, especially if it involves inefficiencies that need to be dealt with. The prevailing thinking seems to indicate that the 'digital divide' India speaks of lies in the polarized difference in access to the Internet for poor people in rural India versus the middle and upper classes in its teeming cities.

The previous gap in wireless feature telephony in our villages versus our cities was largely filled by state-owned Bharat Sanchar Nigam Limited (BSNL). Many stories were then written about India's foray into mobile telephony. They spoke of the 'missed call' culture and how it was used as a rural drumbeat to signal specific events—such as small-time fishermen who used it as a means to communicate the size of their catch while still at sea, thereby allowing their land-based relatives the ability to set a price even before the boats were ashore.

BSNL did not extend its rural networks into the 4G spectrum. This meant that the rural areas remained underserved for a long time by the smart phone 'app' economy that required 4G network technology to work. However, telecom companies have lately been falling over themselves to bridge this digital divide, especially since the entry of Reliance Jio into the market hastened this process.

And predictably, a number of businesses geared to serve this newly online community of 'Bharat' have sprung up, some set up by large corporations, and the rest as start-ups on the lookout for venture capital to market their wares to the millions of Indians now crossing over our current definition of the digital dividing line.

But the truth is that we are fooling ourselves if we think that this is the only digital divide. All of us on the city side of 4G coverage would do very well to look at our new work-from-home or WFH lifestyles. A lot of the work is being done remotely anyhow—as in being done offshore rather than on-site in the US or the UK. This means that shifting work out of the companies and the India-based offices it is agglomerated in and moving the work directly to the same workers who will now instead contract directly with the consuming company is not difficult to accomplish.

Until now, we have seen the rise of a 'marketplace'-oriented business culture only among the bottom-end of service workers such as cab drivers, food delivery and couriers. They provide an interesting sociological test bed for the future, as these marketplace forms of organization begin to replace the current dynamic of employer to employee relationships. We will be contractors, and not employees. And this means a sudden shift to becoming a gig economy worker. This is the real digital divide.

We should not allow the interminable Zoom and webinar meetings we now endure to lull us into a false sense that interacting with other human beings is an integral part of our jobs. The jokes doing the rounds on social media, of workers pouring alcoholic drinks for themselves in receptacles that masquerade as teacups, are not just inane parodies. There is truth in jest. It's probably clear to many of us deep down that expert and continuous human-to-human interchange is not needed for most of our work. So, if we are not primary care doctors, nurses, psychologists or others for whom intense human-to-human contact is the primary point of the job, many of us will find ourselves on the wrong side of the new digital divide.

The sociological impact of working for such marketplaces will follow the history originally established for the management of efficient production at factories. People who now find themselves to be contractors with little rights will organize, and politicians will interfere. Meanwhile, those of us in the muddled middle who will find our work mechanized should go off to either be retrained or retire.

* * *

The benefits of the application of technology in different fields can sometimes only be discovered when taking a risk to invest time and money into research that may take longer periods of time to reach a stage of commercial viability. Consider the concept of start-ups researching how technology can help arrest the ageing process.

A few years ago, I spent a couple of days in Chennai with my then ninety-six-year-old aunt. She was surrounded by a loving family, well cared for, and had kept her physical health for the most part. Unfortunately, her senile dementia had progressed to the point where she was little better than a nine-month-old baby in cognitive function. Being with her was painful.

Her decline was rapid. Less than five years before, she was my mother's companion—and primary care manager—while my mother was going through her own terminal illness. I remember once remarking to my mother how this aunt's *joie de vivre* was astounding for someone who was already a nonagenarian. My mother's response was that this aunt came from a generation that had been toughened by the experience of war while still a young adult. This lady knew how to operate a firearm, a skill she had picked up while being trained as a Malayan–Indian recruit in the Indian National Army (INA) set up by Netaji Subhash Chandra Bose.

Seventy years later, she still had a stentorian voice that she used frequently with the nursing staff assigned to my mother. She had belonged to the Rani of Jhansi regiment, and served until the INA was dissolved after Japan's surrender at the end of World War II—but not before she had lost two of her brothers in battle. Both were officers in the INA, which was the force that did most of Japan's fighting against the British in Burma, all the way up into Imphal in North-east India.

It is probably that rigorous physical training and the medical care she received from my parents later in life that kept up her physical health. But, King Alzheimer came calling regardless, probably finding his way in through the back door that my mother's passing had left open in this lady's mind. I remember her remarking at the time that her 'job was done here' and it was now time for the Almighty to 'send down the lift' for her. Sadly, it seems the call button wasn't working on schedule as she would have liked.

While I was with her in Chennai, I read an article on the website Futurism, which announced that the well-known business accelerator Y Combinator (YC) has launched YC Bio, a funding track specifically for life science companies. Sam Altman, YC's president, announced this new experiment. Due to the size of the biology field, Altman explained that YC thought it made sense to focus on one specific area at a time. He said the company has also found that 'companies working in similar areas get a lot of value from being around each other'. The initial focus will be companies looking to help humans live longer, healthier lives. The attempts here will be too late to help my nonagenarian aunt, but nonetheless, it is encouraging that a leading accelerator/investor is beginning to look at this problem in earnest.

YCC is known for having an innovative method for incubating start-ups. According to its website, it invests $1,20,000 each in a large number of start-ups, twice a year. The start-ups then move to Silicon Valley for three months, during which the accelerator works intensively with them to get the start-up company into the best possible shape to refine its pitch to prospective investors. Each cycle culminates in a 'Demo Day', when the start-ups present their companies to a carefully selected, invite-only audience of investors who might be interested in funding the start-ups' projects. It has funded over 1400 start-ups since 2005, and counts Dropbox, Airbnb and others among its alumni. These are now valued at over $80 billion, according to YC.

The first area of focus for YC Bio is 'health span' and age-related disease. Health span is the idea that medicine should not just help people live longer, but also allow those people to enjoy good health and a high quality of life over the course of their years. 'We think there's an enormous opportunity to help people live healthier for longer, and that it could be one of the best ways to address our healthcare crisis,' Altman wrote in his blog post announcing YC Bio.

According to Futurism, like the YC AI track, which funds companies focusing on AI, companies participating in YC Bio will first go through the accelerator's regular batch before receiving their offer. Like YC's AI track, instead of the standard YC deal of

$1,20,000 in exchange for a 7 per cent ownership, YC Bio companies will receive an offer between $5,00,000 and $1 million for a larger piece of ownership.

This additional funding beyond the seed stage is critical to start-ups that are focused on deep science and deep tech. There is an investing lacuna across the entire world of the sciences; start-ups can find seed funding through grants but fall into a crevasse soon afterwards. Critical follow-on funding for series A and series B rounds of capital injection are often absent. Investors fear deep science and deep tech start-ups since their route to commercialization seems longer than that of start-ups based solely on digitizing existing business models.

The investors' fear is unfounded. Some months ago, I wrote of Jeanette Wing, previously a senior executive at Microsoft and now a data science engineering professor at Columbia University. Wing recounts her days at Microsoft, where she realized that the company had stepped in to fund research where traditional funding did not exist. The role that Microsoft played in funding data science research ten or twelve years ago was pivotal to the advances we see today. Wing says she used to remind the CEO and CFO of that firm that they would not be making certain revenues had they not invested in the space a decade ago. It is good to see the investing world slowly waking up to start-ups in science.

***

It is a known fact that technology will replace many jobs and improve the efficiency of an industry. But as I have droned on earlier in this book, one must understand how this will work and what the implications are, such as in the case of how mutual funds can be affected by new algorithmic models.

Algorithmic or automated trading refers to using a computer program that automatically submits trades to an exchange without any human intervention. This ensures that human beings' emotions are not triggered while making the investment or trading calls and, instead, the computer program is able to place trades with a level of speed and precision that a human could not hope to achieve.

Algorithmic trading is popular among institutional investors in India and covers 35–40 per cent of the turnover on our exchanges. Early in 2018, the Securities and Exchange Board of India (SEBI) had probed the algorithmic trading platform available on the NSE and had found that some investors had unfair access to market information and trading systems. Since then, SEBI has instituted a stronger regulatory framework for such trading.

Writing for the *Mint*, a successful business daily in India, Nilanjana Chakraborty also dissected what such algorithmic trading meant for the retail investor. She concluded that the technology to do this is not easily accessible to small-time investors, who would find the costs of setting up a separate set of servers to perform such trading too high. Though there are no guidelines for retail investors, some brokerage firms do offer algorithmic trading as a product. Last year, it was reported that Sebi is likely to put out guidelines for algorithmic trading for retail investors; these are still awaited. According to Chakraborty, it is important to keep in mind that algorithmic trading is a market (trading) strategy and is not meant for long-term investors.

However, globally, traditional asset management could well be an industry ripe for technological disruption by using smart algorithms. Algorithms armed with computing power can extract value from big data by recognizing and unearthing patterns from the ever-changing construct of financial markets, thereby making the human 'investment officer' obsolete.

I spoke recently with Mazhar Khan, founder of a start-up still in 'stealth' mode, who intends to apply the principles of algorithmic modelling to building a fund portfolio for long-term investors. Khan has more than two decades of experience and has managed advisory assets of $2 billion while working for multinational private banks. He says that the inconsistency in the performance of equity mutual funds available in the market today means it is difficult to construct investment portfolios for clients.

Spiva or 'S&P Indices Versus Active' is a scorecard published by S&P Dow Jones Indices that compares the performance of market indices versus actively managed mutual funds. Khan cites a study by Spiva that shows that 85–90 per cent of US equity mutual fund schemes have underperformed their benchmarks across 3-, 5-, and 10-year horizons. He says that this underperformance is not restricted to the US and is also prevalent in Europe and in emerging markets. As markets become more volatile and unpredictable with a high velocity of information flow, performance consistency seems to be no more within the realm of traditional mutual fund managers. Over the last four years, more than $4 trillion has moved out of the $18 trillion US mutual fund industry into passively managed index funds and exchange-traded funds or ETFs.

Khan has been on a course of exploration in behavioural science, financial theories and quantitative models, the result of which, he claims, is an algorithm-based investment model suited to the global long-term investor. According to him, the model is grounded in the fundamental performance of companies and in the behavioural constructs of stock price movements. These behavioural constructs are not based on technical analysis, but on the long-term statistical data behind stock performance. By contrast, pure algorithmic trading focuses on short-term market anomalies or arbitrage opportunities.

Considering the speed of development in AI, Khan believes that large-scale analysis of historical fundamental performance and behavioural constructs is now technologically feasible. Moreover, the absence of asset managers and their minions from such 'algorithmically managed' investments will mean that fund costs are kept low for the investor. The secret sauce will lie in the algorithmic model's construct. Khan says that industry leaders such as Larry Fink of BlackRock, Inc. and Paul Tudor Jones of

Tudor Investment Corp. have seen the light and are opening up more of their portfolios to algorithmic long-term investment. The Indian asset management industry, on the other hand, he says, has been extremely slow and hesitant to adapt to the changing trends shaping global markets.

For his start-up, the technology roadmap he plans is to scale his algorithms to provide a robust mechanism to innovate and roll out multiple thematic 'quant' and 'smart Beta' strategies that can be offered as funds, ETFs and index funds, depending on the maturity of specific buyers.

He intends to go to the market approaching both institutional investors, such as family offices and pension funds, as well as small- to medium-sized funds, including existing registered investment companies and 'long-only' hedge funds.

The start-up's idea seems a fine one, but the actual technological and operational execution of it is where success will lie. This will be Khan's real challenge.

* * *

There isn't only one specific area in which technology can change an industry. Consider the development of new car batteries, which is likely to come to fruition before automated driving tech.

Intel Corp. plans to use India as a test bed for creating algorithms to promote automated driving. These algorithms, when refined over time with ever greater amounts of correctly labelled data, will supposedly take over the functions of controlling and driving a machine so that the functions are performed by electronics instead of humans.

Every big tech company, ride-hailing service, as well as every automobile company worth its salt, is trying to be the first when it comes to self-driven vehicles. The technologies that underlie this worthy effort are myriad. Smart cameras, sonar technology, the Internet of Things, ML, AI—name the buzzword and it's being bandied about. Billions of dollars of capital investment in these technologies are being burnt at the same time. Cities and local governments are exercising their legislative powers in different ways to ensure the safety of people on their roads.

I have no doubt that we will get to the point where we see autonomous vehicles in the foreseeable future—yes, even on Indian roads—but there will be many hiccups on the way. I would bet that we will see these advances before the gasoline-powered automobile gives way to its nemesis—the 'clean' electric vehicle (EV).

Many scientific researchers and start-ups are working on the next generation of battery, which they hope will be more effective than today's standard lithium-ion batteries. Some are working on 'solid-state' batteries which don't have any liquid inside and, hence, will be less sensitive to fluctuations in temperature. Others are working on supercapacitor-based solutions. One such start-up is India's Gegadyne Energy. Today's supercapacitors have low energy density when compared to lithium-ion and are expensive and bulky, and so their use is limited to being deployed alongside lithium-ion batteries in a hybrid solution to manage peak requirements.

However, supercapacitors hold out promise, as they have much shorter charge and discharge rates. I spoke recently with Jubin Varghese, the CEO of Gegadyne, who claims that supercapacitors also have enhanced life cycles and can be charged more than 1 million times. Gegadyne claims that some of its batteries can be charged in seconds, but used for hours. What is more, the start-up company claims to have arrived at a solution that combines the best characteristics of a common battery with those of supercapacitors. According to Varghese, this is because of advances in material science. He and his collaborators have invented a new form of 'carbon-slurry' as the main material in the company's devices and have already applied for or received patent protection for their technology.

In a vindication of Gegadyne's approach, Tesla has agreed to buy US energy storage company Maxwell Technologies in a deal that valued the specialist battery and capacitor maker at $218 million. Maxwell describes itself as a global leader in the development and manufacturing of energy and power delivery solutions. The acquisition is being described by analysts as a perfect fit for Musk's ambitious EV project, as a low-risk bet on lowering battery costs and boosting battery performance.

It appears that we might have a breakthrough in a battery solution for EVs long before we have perfect self-driving cars, electric or otherwise. Assuming, of course, that the EVs' on-board software will allow occupants access and egress from the vehicle!

* * *

The potential of new tech may be exciting, but one must keep in mind the physical barriers that prevent theory from being put into practice. Consider the example of deep tech and its high computing power requirements.

It appears that many of the deep tech algorithms the world is excited about will run into physical barriers before they reach their true promise. Take Bitcoin. A cryptocurrency based on blockchain technology, it has a sophisticated algorithm that grows in complexity, as very few new bitcoins are minted—through a digital process called 'mining'. There is a fixed total number of bitcoin, and the amount that remains to be mined is an infinitesimal fraction of what the original number was.

Bitcoin and other cryptocurrencies are dependent on users having 'wallets' which they use to store their hoard of cryptocurrency. These are then traded through the bitcoin network, and with institutions that are willing to transfer the contents of these bitcoin wallets into cash—or allow bitcoin to be transferred to their own wallets for purchases or other settlements. These cryptocurrency wallets are notoriously unsafe, and online hackers devise ever new methods of getting into people's cryptowallets to siphon off their contents.

Bitcoin's assurance of validity is achieved by its 'proving' algorithm, which is designed to continually increase in mathematical complexity—and hence the computing power needed to process it—every time a bitcoin is mined. Individual miners are continually doing work to assess the validity of each bitcoin transaction and confirm whether it adheres to the cryptocurrency's rules. They earn small amounts of new bitcoins for their efforts. The complexity of getting several miners to agree on the same history of transactions (and thereby validate them) is managed by the same miners who try outpacing one another to create a valid 'block'. And since the amount of bitcoin left for these miners to fight over is so much smaller than it was at the cryptocurrency's inception, proving the algorithm continues to become harder and harder. In simple mathematical terms, this is a number that continuously approaches the total number of bitcoin, but never actually will (an asymptote). The gap between this number and the total number of bitcoin will never be equal, but the difference between them will become ever smaller—all the way to infinity. The concept is not dissimilar from imperfect fractions such as the value of Pi which is 3.1417....... without end. As a result, the algorithm keeps getting harder and harder for mining each new bitcoin. The computing power needed to simply make the mathematical calculation is now truly absurd—it uses more power than many small countries!

The machines that perform this work consume huge amounts of energy. According to Digiconomist.net, each transaction uses almost 544KWh of electrical energy—enough to provide for the average US household for almost three weeks. The total energy consumption of the bitcoin network alone is about 64TWh, enough to provide for all the energy needs of Switzerland. The website also tracks the carbon footprint and electronic waste left behind by bitcoin, which are both startlingly high. This exploitation of resources is unsustainable in the long run, and directly impacts global warming. At a more mundane level, the costs of mining bitcoin can outstrip the rewards.

But cryptocurrencies are not the world's only hogs of computing power. Many AI 'deep learning neural' algorithms also place crushing demands on the planet's digital processing capacity.

A 'neural network' attempts to mimic the functioning of the human brain and nervous system in AI learning models. There are many of these. The two most widely used are recursive neural networks, which develop a memory pattern, and convolutional neural networks, which develop spatial reasoning. The first is used for tasks such as language translation, and the second for image processing. These use enormous computing power, as do other AI neural network models that help with deep learning.

Frenetic research has been going into new chip architectures for these to handle the ever-increasing complexity of AI models more efficiently. Today's computers are binary, meaning they depend on the two simple states of a transistor bit—which could be either on or off, and thus either a 0 or 1 in binary notation. Newer chips try to achieve efficiency through other architectures. This will ostensibly help binary computers execute algorithms more efficiently. These chips are designed as graphic-processing units, since they are more capable of dealing with AI's demands than central processing units, which are the mainstay of most devices.

In a parallel attempt to get beyond binary computing, firms such as DWave, Google and IBM are working on a different class of machines called quantum computers, which make use of the so-called 'qubit', with each qubit able to hold 0 and 1 values simultaneously. This enhances computing power. The problem with these, though, is that they are far from seeing widespread adoption. First off, they are not yet sophisticated enough to manage today's AI models efficiently, and second, they need to be maintained at temperatures that are close to absolute zero (–273° Celsius). This refrigeration, in turn, uses up enormous amounts of electrical energy.

Clearly, advances in both binary chip design and quantum computing are not keeping pace with the increasing sophistication of deep tech algorithms.

In a research paper published by IEEE Spectrum, Neil Thompson of the Massachusetts Institute of Technology and others analyse five widely-used AI application areas and show that advances in each of these fields of use come at a huge cost, since they are reliant on massive increases in computing capability. The five areas that Thompson et al. examined are 1) image classification, 2) object detection, 3) question answering, 4) named entity recognition, and 5) machine translation. The authors argue that extrapolating this reliance forward reveals that current progress is rapidly becoming economically, technically and environmentally unsustainable.

Sustained progress in these applications will require changes to their deep learning algorithms and/or moving away from deep learning to other machine learning models that allow greater efficiency in their use of computing capability. The authors further argue that we are currently in an era where improvements in hardware performance are slowing, which means that this shift away from deep neural networks is now all the more urgent.

Thompson et al. argue that the economic, environmental and purely technical costs of providing all this additional computing power will soon constrain deep learning and a range of applications, making the achievement of key milestones impossible, if current trajectories hold.

We are designing increasingly sophisticated algorithms, but we don't yet have computers that are sophisticated enough to match their demands efficiently. Without significant changes in how AI models are built, the usefulness of AI and other forms of deep tech is likely to hit a wall soon.

Chapter 13

Musings for the Originator or 'Cross-Pollinator'

In 2016, as bitcoin had begun to gain ascendance many years after its original debut, I was asked by a senior banker what bitcoin and blockchain were. Another friend, a doctor, insisted that she knew what blockchain was just as well as she knew Facebook, Instagram and other social media 'technology'. The fact that someone with so many degrees and many years of experience thinks that blockchain is a social media technology boggles the mind.

Notice how one was willing to accept his lack of knowledge, while the other only too willingly displayed her ignorance! The banker showed enough humility to ask about something most people would have simply assumed he knew about. But he didn't, and he had the guts to ask. This is acceptance at its best. The banker's attitude allowed him to accept the seemingly 'unacceptable' (the fact that a banker might not know about financial technology).

The doctor, who works in a back-room speciality where patients don't get to choose their doctors, has probably led her life without paying much attention to feedback. She is unable to accept that she might not know everything simply because her expertise has not yet been challenged. She certainly could use the tricks we discussed in Chapter 11.

Are you in the doctor's position or in the banker's? You may as well be honest with yourself. If you don't know something, it's best to ask. The only stupid question is the one that you didn't ask.

Now we've got that out of the way, here is a superficial explanation of what blockchain and bitcoin really are:

Blockchain is the formalization—through Internet technology—of a process that most people intuitively understand—the promissory note—and its dark side, the 'grey market' system. Blockchain technology was underfunded because few still understand what it means. At least until 2016, according to the *Wall Street Journal* and research firms familiar with VC funding, only about 2 to 3 per cent of the total new VC funding of about $20 billion in financial services goes to blockchain.

If I issue a promissory note to pay the bearer a sum of, say, $20,000, then I have no choice but to cough up when the holder of the note demands payment. After all, I want to continue to keep my reputation among my business associates and their extended network that I can be trusted. In a grey market exchange, the promissory note is notional. It is often converted into different currencies while it passes through the hands of individuals. Each individual in the chain trusts that the next one will deliver on the promise to pass on the same $20,000 until it reaches its final recipient.

In short, it is a clearing system. The $20,000 (or any other amount initially defined by the first two transacting parties) is the defined 'block' and the hands it passes through form the 'chain'. All these hands recognize that the value of the block is $20,000 and not some different amount. And they all have the ability to simultaneously write down in their account books (or ledgers) what each unique block is worth.

Blockchain technology is also known as Distributed Ledger Technology or DLT. It allows for instant recognition of the exact size of the block by all transacting parties in the chain since the block is simultaneously updated on all their databases (or ledgers/account books). The block also has unique security features that do not allow tampering with its definition. In addition, the technology assures that each block's movements across the chain have the ability to be verified by all parties in the chain.

The impact of this is revolutionary. It creates instant trust since all participants in the blockchain are naturally interested in keeping transactions sacrosanct. Information sharing, value transfer and the recording of transactions in a decentralized, secure, digital environment is what distinguishes this technology from today's clearing house transactions. Today's transactions require a trusted central clearing house like a bank, or credit card issuer such as Visa or MasterCard.

So, what then, is bitcoin, and what are the other cryptocurrencies? Cryptocurrencies try to fashion themselves as money—as a medium of exchange for goods and services and as a store of value. Bitcoin is an attempt by a firm, using blockchain technology, to create a set of shares in a trading entity that had an initial set value and fixed number (much like the face value and number of shares offered in an IPO). The firm hopes that these shares will become the medium of exchange through which people trade goods and services. Since the number of shares (or coins) is fixed, the firm hopes that demand for them goes up over a period of time as more and more people use its cryptocurrency to settle their transactions. The bet is that each bitcoin's value goes up stratospherically since there will never ever be any more bitcoins issued. Other cryptocurrencies like ethereum work on similar lines.

Most countries still don't understand the cryptocurrency process fully. But regulation will certainly catch up. In June 2018, the Securities and Exchange Commission (SEC) of the

US recognized that blockchain/DLT—the parent technology of cryptocurrencies—is likely to revolutionize e-commerce but stated publicly that bitcoin and ethereum—the two mediums that have most highly valued presence in the crypto market—are not securities. However, the SEC has said that Initial Coin Offerings, where new cryptocurrencies are launched, probably fit the definition of a security investment. This is because they contain an implied promise that the issuing firm will do something with proprietary technology or tools to raise the value of investors' holdings. The natural conclusion from this is that the SEC will seek to regulate new cryptocurrencies coming into the market but will stay away from established ones.

That said, bodies like the SEC only cover the regulation of a part of trade and commerce. Money supply might not be a topic for the SEC, but it certainly comes under the purview of other fiscal departments of a country's government. Sovereign governments don't like allowing companies to issue their own coin and will eventually regulate such systems. For instance, Victorian England stopped allowing the East India Company to issue its own coinage in India. That last intervention took a war for Independence in 1857 before the British Crown stepped in. Today's governments are unlikely to wait for war to break out before they regulate something that affects their ability to issue and guarantee currency. Facebook's Libra has fallen flat due to governmental opposition. China has recently outlawed all cryptocurrency. India has also now passed its own laws about how cryptocurrencies may be used by Indian residents. Apart from punitive taxes on transactions where residents make capital gains on cryptocurrency, the government has directed the Reserve Bank of India to float and manage a fiat cryptocurrency, thereby cutting out private players. The COVID-19 pandemic has seen a huge surge and then a fall in bitcoin, but it has as many detractors as it has takers.

However, all the issued bitcoins haven't been released yet, as I referenced in Chapter 12. A small number of them remain unreleased and can be earned through a process called mining.

The mining process is one where some members of the bitcoin community independently verify whether each new transaction set up under bitcoin's blockchain is genuine. Their reward for doing so is the ability to earn a few bitcoins for each verified transaction. As of the end of 2021, the total number of bitcoins in existence has exceeded 18.3 million. Approximately 4 million bitcoins are lost forever. The total number of bitcoins that will ever be produced stands at 21 million. Only 13 million bitcoins are in circulation or stashed away in wallets.

This verification process has become infinitely more difficult as the store of unreleased bitcoins dwindles. Miners now have to use extensive computing power and vast amounts of electricity to run their computers to de-encrypt and verify each new transaction. Some estimates already say that the energy used by bitcoin miners exceeds the entire energy use of many small countries put together. At some point, the process of mining will become futile, as the store of unreleased bitcoins gets down to close to zero. At that point, the costs associated with mining bitcoins, in terms of electricity and computing power, would have gone up way beyond economically viable levels. At that point, the mining system will most likely die a natural death.

Observers think that there are three possibilities for how bitcoin will develop. The first, and most unlikely, is that governments will step aside and allow cryptocurrencies to become the fiat currencies in each country. They base this possibility on the fact that El Salvador has already done so. (This is not surprising since El Salvador does not have its own currency—it was already using the US dollar as its official currency when it decided to also include bitcoin.) The second is that bitcoin and others will vanish since they will never become a method for paying for daily necessities—meaning they will never exhibit the classic definition of money as a medium of exchange. The third is that fiat currencies will continue to be the main medium of exchange, but bitcoin and others like it will become 'stores of value', much like gold is today.

As an aside, the Russian invasion of Ukraine in February 2022 saw another interesting use case for cryptocurrencies. Friends of Ukraine have started using cryptocurrency as a way to crowdfund the Ukrainian war effort. This was after the organization Patreon, a leading platform for crowdfunding on the Internet (and therefore a centralized node in the money movement network), inexplicably kicked off the non-profit Ukrainian foundation 'Come Back Alive', which was supporting Ukraine's military effort. Patreon nixed the foundation around 24 February 2022, citing its own policy on 'harmful and illegal activities'. This timing was inexplicable, especially since the non-profit had been active on the platform for years. The beauty of cryptocurrencies decentralized ledgers allowed Ukrainian supporters to continue to raise cash for the country's war effort.

Fiat currencies used to be pegged to gold until about a century ago, after which most countries abandoned the gold standard. That move, however, did not stop people trading in gold and even using it as a store of value during times of economic uncertainty. This practice continues, since people still move to gold when their countries experience hyperinflation, such as Venezuela has in the recent past with its fiat currency. The skyrocketing price of gold during the COVID-19 crisis has proven this yet again.

Gold, like bitcoin, also experiences booms and busts in its price, usually based on how much of it is being bought up as a store of value. In my mind, the only likely scenarios are the second or the third. Also, between the two last scenarios, since gold already exists as an alternate store of value, the store of value outcome is the less likely one. I realize that making predictions is a mug's game, but my bet is that cryptocurrencies will eventually fizzle out.

Economists seem to agree. Eric Budish, of the University of Chicago's Booth School of Business, has published a working paper entitled 'The Economic Limits of Bitcoin and the Blockchain'. His principal argument is that all money works via trust. Banks, which certify and act as clearing houses for fiat currency transactions, have built up trust over time, so each new transaction is very cheap to complete. Bitcoin's process runs on a decentralized network, and there's no trusted intermediary. Trust has to be re-established each time there is a transaction by people from the mining community. As we will see later, the costs of mining are already in the stratosphere, and won't be coming down any time soon.

My suggestion then, is that you try to understand how the parent technology—the blockchain or DLT—may affect you or your firm. DLT's value is not restricted to money alone. Potential applications for blockchain/DLT include supply chain management, real estate contracts, intellectual property rights, degree/diploma verification and so on.

Think through areas where your business's operations do not need to use the intermediaries they currently use in order to transact. Think out of the box—are there other areas, such as your firm's supply chain or records management where blockchain can be used? Can you help your organization or team learn and understand the change? Can you organize the change? Can you help build it? Do you know where you or your organization may be threatened with disruption? Remember, all one needs to do is to clearly see where the middleman can be cut out.

* * *

Blockchain has also created a new frontier called Web 3.0. Proponents of Web 3.0 claim that they will 'democratize' the Internet by providing decentralized recognition of web page addresses (domain names). Ostensibly, these web 3.0 addresses will become the fundamental way in which non-fungible tokens (or NFTs) are used across the Internet. They will use blockchain as the underlying technology. To see how this could revolutionize the Internet, one must understand how domain names are currently controlled across the Internet.

Many news articles have already warned about the fact that the US losing primacy in the digital revolution now taking place can have serious effects on cybercrime and warfare. Interestingly enough, the US gave up its hegemony over the Internet just a few years ago to a not-for-profit (but still US-based) group called Icann. Icann, or the Internet Corporation for Assigned Names and Numbers, now manages the master keys for the DNS backbone of the Internet. There are only seven individuals from all over the globe who actually hold the master keys to the Internet—the DNS registry—and a further seven individuals as back-up. These fourteen individuals have been chosen carefully to make sure that no one country is over-represented.

Each of these fourteen keys are actually physical metal keys to safety deposit boxes, which in turn carry smartcards, which then in turn activate a machine that creates a new master key for the Internet. Icann holds highly secure meetings four times each year during which it conducts an elaborate ceremony called the 'Root Signing Ceremony' that can quite literally form the stuff that spy movies are made of, with windowless rooms and steel doors that require biometric scans, PIN codes and smartcards to open. During these ceremonies, the master key that was in existence for the past three months is scrapped, and a new cryptographic key is generated by a single high-security computer, which is then uploaded to servers like the ones owned by Dyn, dictating who owns .com, .net, .in, .org and others.

No, this is not part of the script for a James Bond movie. It is how the Internet actually works. One can't even begin to fathom what might happen if one of these 'ceremonies' was somehow compromised, and the master key came into the hands of criminals or terrorists. The recent attack mainly affected Dyn, which is only one of the companies that controls domain names—there are several others like it. But control over the master key would mean that all firms who provide domain name services could be compromised, thereby annihilating the Internet as we know it.

No one really knows who put Icann in charge. Some claim that it's the 'online community' while most others realize that it could only have been the US agency that was originally entrusted with this responsibility. Many other countries, such as Brazil, Russia and the EU have questioned this and have suggested that it be put under the auspices of the UN. It seems the view I have expressed in some of my columns about the need for a global body like the UN to monitor and manage both the security as well as the equitable distribution of technology has more takers than I first thought. Web 3.0 is an attempt to remove this centralization of domain name registries and the hegemony of Icann.

Web 3.0 depends on blockchain, and as we have already seen, blockchain is a peer-to-peer network and does not need a central body to verify (or issue) domain names. The impact of this could be really far reaching and upend the Internet as we know it today. Its supporters today say that Web3 is a decentralized version of the Internet where platforms and apps are built and owned by users. Unlike Web2 (the current web), which is dominated by centralized platforms such as Google, Apple and Facebook, Web3 will use blockchain, crypto and NFTs to transfer power back to the *aam janata* or common man of the Internet community. I for one support it, and believe that Web 3.0 will take hold soon.

Unsurprisingly, there are others who don't share my views. These detractors say that all Web 3.0 is going to do is to move control of the Internet from today's behemoths such as Facebook and Google over to another set of behemoths. And, of course, that today's behemoths will morph themselves enough to also dominate Web 3.0. They quote studies (by the *Financial Times* and others) that show that today's blockchain, NFT and crypto market are already controlled by only very few firms/individuals. For instance, 9 per cent of accounts control over 80 per cent of the ethereum cryptocurrency, which in total is now valued at more than US$40 billion. Similarly, the top 2 per cent of accounts own and control 95 per cent of the US$800 billion supply of bitcoin, and that 0.1 per cent of bitcoin miners are responsible for all new bitcoin output.

Let's see how this space plays out, but as an executive today, you need to be extremely watchful of the new Web 3.0 space, whether or not its promised 'democracy' comes to pass or whether all we are seeing is a recentralization of value in the hands of a few.

***

Decentralized Finance (or DeFi, as it's commonly called in the tech industry) is gaining prominence. DeFi allows apps that can create financial instruments using cryptocurrencies such as bitcoin and ethereum.

A largely unregulated part of the economy, DeFi has exploded in tandem with the demand for cryptocurrencies like bitcoin and ethereum. For now, the ecosystem is populated primarily by people who are comfortable with crypto—with all its risk and legal uncertainty. I say legal uncertainty since, as I have discussed elsewhere in this book, countries are not comfortable with private players issuing their own currencies, let alone derivative transactions or other financial instruments based on such digital (crypto) currencies, which is what DeFi apps look to do.

The DeFi world includes apps that create all sorts of financial instruments, which are not simply new cryptocurrencies. DeFi represents a concerted, crowdsourced effort to put cryptocurrencies to work, offering people financial reasons to hold crypto beyond merely speculating on price movements. Because of the explosion in DeFi apps, crypto is finally not just about a new gold or a new kind of money; it represents a way to structure financial transactions that are far more sophisticated. Each new app debuting in the DeFi world seems to be cooking up pieces of an entire financial system based solely on the crypto world, and not on currencies such as the dollar or the rupee, which the older ones among you and I understand better.

Apart from just an alternate way to pay and settle immediate cash transactions, and to as act as a store of value, DeFi unlocks the potential of digital currencies by allowing them to be morphed into financial instruments. At the first level of abstraction, these can be simple forward contracts on cash settlements, such as letters of credit used in the import/export world.

But this sort of use is simple. In the DeFi world, there are several apps taking shape. Some of the more popular ones include apps such as PoolTogether, which have 'loss-less' lotteries using ethereum's smart contract layer, which allows developers anywhere in the world to publish decentralized applications with limitless functionality. Unsurprisingly, this tool has been quick to provide value to the gambling industry, which stands to benefit enormously by removing trust from both the players and middlemen. The best way to describe loss-less lotteries in Indian parlance is to liken it to the kind of chit fund that randomly picks the winner of the pot for the month, rather than by using a monthly auction methodology to determine the taker of the pot. Like chit funds, these apps have formed an alternate banking system for savings and loans, but they are based solely on a cryptocurrency and not the country's legal tender. And like chit funds, they are not insured by any country's deposit insurance mechanisms.

If you are a speculator rather than an investor, check out legal DeFi by all means.

But these apps are skating on thin ice. Governments do not like private organizations creating alternate cash. China has recently become yet another country that has outlawed all crypto transactions, just before the Evergrande crisis broke out. This action will certainly put a crimp on capital flight from China. Other countries are mulling similar moves.

***

Consider the use of neuroeconomics in the corporate world. When I was a postgraduate student, the top practitioners in economics did not give much credence to behavioural economists. It was thought that they could not provide sufficient replicable empirical mathematical evidence, and so they were relegated to less prominent schools and universities.

The modelling of decisions made by a typical 'rational' human being, which was the cornerstone of most empirical schools, was but a contrivance used to arrive at mathematical proofs that were presented in top journals, such as the *Journal of Financial Economics*. Rare is the student of economics who has never considered that this rational human being is, in fact, just a myth. Such scepticism has been proven right over the last few years.

The beauty of any seminal thought in economics lies in its ability to engender a reaction in the reader that goes along the lines of, 'Yes, of course, that's true. I knew that!'

One such was the theory of agency costs, first promulgated by William Meckling and Michael Jensen, who were both professors at the University of Rochester at the time. I have referenced these 'agency costs' earlier in Chapter 8 while discussing the nature of the modern company or firm as an organization which builds itself around the delivery of value to its customers. Agency costs laid out a simple economic truth that an owner's agents were less likely than owners of the business to run the business efficiently. In other words, managers (agents) needed to be compensated in much the same way as owners (shareholders). This led to the liberal use of stock options and grants in the compensation schemes for senior managers of a firm, thereby strongly linking executive pay with stock-price performance. This compensation technique is now widely used the world over.

The emergence of behavioural economics has shown that reliance on a single measure, such as a commission, is naive and that the average rational human being is a myth. Lately, the application of computer science to this field has given rise to a new field called 'neuroeconomics', which tries to model and instigate human action. We have seen some of these models being used to drive political action, especially through the subversion of social media platforms, but these models are also equally applicable to the management of large businesses.

Software giants such as SalesForceDotCom (SFDC) have been managing the lead generation and sales process space and providing consistent, streamlined methods to push the sales process along. These are template-driven, but can be tweaked with the help of neuroeconomics to deliver much more effective results.

The availability of information to salespeople is known to spark a strong 'intent to act'. However, this in itself may not result in action. Information overload and indecision often go hand in hand. This leaves sales managers frustrated over their failure to achieve 'desirable' outcomes.

Confronting this last-mile problem involves the embedding of algorithmic behaviour design to ensure that sales personnel consistently follow through on targets. Getting an individual employee to act requires recognizing both the blocks that inhibit action and the motivations that initiate it.

* * *

The development of new technology can come from a variety of different places. Here is an example of how molecular biology can help drive the development of new technology. One of the main contributors to making AI a powerful tool today is the advanced level of computing we have arrived at. Most of us hold smartphones in our hands that have more computing capability than it took to land Neil Armstrong on the moon fifty years ago. Efforts are on to keep increasing this capability, and the advances researchers are seeking to make in quantum computing is one of these.

The other axis is the inexorable rise in data that we cough up, some of it voluntarily and a lot of it involuntarily, for the benefit of the big tech companies that now control our world. This data gets produced by our ever-increasing use of the Internet. This has caused a phenomenon called 'data inundation', where firms are collecting large amounts of data on their customers and operations, but don't quite yet know what to do with it. Meanwhile, according to the advisory Ark Invest, such data is predicted to grow to 44 zettabytes by the end of next year, and the deficit of computer storage space that can contain all this data will grow to 500 per cent, meaning that most of it can't be stored and will become useless.

Molecular biology may come to the rescue. It turns out that Mother Nature's DNA is the data storage mechanism to beat all computers. According to *New Scientist*, 1 gram of DNA can hold up to 455 exabytes of data (there are 1000 exabytes in 1 zettabyte). This means all 44 zettabytes of data produced by the end of next year can actually be stored on just 97 grams of DNA.

There are four types of molecules that make up DNA, which forms pairs. To encode information on DNA, scientists programme the pairs into 1s and 0s—the same binary language that encodes digital data. This concept is not new; scientists at Harvard University encoded a book on to DNA in 2012, but up to now, it has been difficult to retrieve the information stored in DNA.

Now, researchers from Microsoft Corp. and the University of Washington claim to have demonstrated the first fully automated system to store and retrieve data in manufactured 'synthetic' DNA—a key step in moving the technology out of the research lab and into commercial data centres. Under helpful conditions, DNA can last much longer than current computer storage technologies that can degrade in a few years. As we know, some DNA has managed to persist in less than ideal storage conditions for tens of thousands of years in the bones of early humans, such as the one found recently in deep freeze in the Alps.

Information is stored in synthetic DNA molecules created in a lab, not DNA taken from living beings, and can be encrypted before it is sent to the system. While sophisticated machines such as synthesizers and sequencers already perform key parts of the process, many of the intermediate steps until now have required manual labour in the research lab. This would not be viable in a commercial setting, but work is being done to automate this.

The automated DNA data storage system uses software developed by the Microsoft and University of Washington team to convert the 1s and 0s of digital data into the four molecular building blocks of DNA. Before a file can be written to DNA, its data must first be translated from 1s and 0s into what are known as the As, Cs, Ts, and Gs of DNA.

The team claims that it then used inexpensive, largely off-the-shelf lab equipment to flow the necessary liquids and chemicals into a synthesizer that builds manufactured snippets of DNA to push them into a storage vessel. When the system needed to retrieve the information, it added other chemicals to accurately prepare the DNA and used microfluidic pumps to push the liquids into other parts of the system that 'read' the DNA sequences and converted them back to information that a computer could understand.

The goal of the above project was not to prove how fast or inexpensively the system could work, according to the researchers, but simply to demonstrate that automation is possible. While a paltry five bytes in twenty-one hours is not commercially viable, the researchers say there exists a precedent for many orders of magnitude improvement in such data storage. Also, unlike silicon-based computing systems, DNA-based storage and computing systems have to use liquids to move molecules around. And fluids are inherently different from silicon's electrons and require entirely new engineering solutions.

Nonetheless, this research opens up a fascinating new flank at the intersection of biology and computing.

* * *

Innovation in technology is not just about reinventing the wheel and inventing new technology but also the ability to improve the efficiency of current technology, as is the case with the application of quantum physics to technology. All of today's computing takes its root from the world of bits, where a transistor bit, which lies at the heart of any computing chip, can only be in one of two electrical states: on or off. When on, the bit takes on a value of '1' and when off, it takes on a value of '0', constraining the bit to only one of two (binary) values. All tasks performed by a computer-like device, whether a simple calculator or a sophisticated computer, are constrained by this binary rule.

Eight bits make up what is called a byte. Today, our computing is based on increasing the number of bytes into kilobytes, megabytes, gigabytes and so on. All computing advances we have had thus far, including artificially intelligent programmes and driverless cars, are ultimately reduced to the binary world of the bit.

This is a natural extension of western thought; for centuries, western philosophy has followed the principles of Aristotelian logic, which is based on the law of identity (A is A), the law of contradiction (A is not non-A), and the law of the excluded middle (A cannot be both A and non-A at the same time, just as non-A cannot be both non-A and A at the same time).

This axiom is so deeply imbedded in our thinking that to us, a statement that something is both A and non-A at the same time seems absurd. Paradoxically, however, the idea that something can be both A and non-A at the same time, the crucible of most eastern philosophical thought, is the essence of quantum computing. This idea was first proposed in 1985 by British physicist David Deutsch but has gained currency only recently.

With quantum computing, which I discussed briefly in Chapter 12, information is held in qubits that can exist in two states at the same time. Incredibly, a qubit can store a '0' and '1' simultaneously. If you build two qubits, they can hold four values at once—11, 10, 01, and 00. So, adding on more qubits can greatly increase the computing capability of such a machine. IBM now has a new machine with a 50-qubit processor (at least at the time I wrote this).

The logical extension of quantum computing is a quantum Internet, where computers don't just compute in isolation, they also communicate with one another. Scientists are now working on how a quantum Internet might work. To accomplish this, they are beginning by providing a vision of fundamentally new technology protocols to enable network communications between any two quantum computing machines on Earth. They say that such a quantum Internet will—in synergy with the 'classical' Internet that we have today—connect quantum computers in order to achieve unparalleled capabilities that are impossible today.

As with any radical new technology, it is hard to predict all uses of the future quantum Internet. In a recent issue of *Science* magazine, theoretical physicist Stephanie Wehner et al. say that several major applications for the quantum Internet have already been identified, including secure communication, secure identification, achieving efficient agreement on distributed data as well as secure access to remote quantum computers in the cloud.

Obviously, the ability of a quantum Internet to transmit qubits that are fundamentally different from classical '1' and '0' bits is what is paramount. According to the scientists' paper, qubits also cannot be copied, and any attempt to do so can be detected. This makes qubits well suited for security applications. At the same time, the authors feel that the transmission of qubits requires radical new concepts and technology as well as concerted efforts in physics, computer science and engineering to succeed. They propose the need for a unified framework for quantum Internet researchers.

The authors say that although it is hard to predict what the exact components of a future quantum Internet will be, it is likely that we will see the birth of the first multinodal quantum network in the next few years. If so, all the ideas that so far only exist on paper may indeed turn out to be the dawn of a functional, large-scale quantum Internet.

* * *

Consider the proliferation of new chip architectures for AI. Most advances in AI have so far been confined to software. Today's AI computer programs are vast users of data. They sift through this data and use methods such as pattern recognition. For instance, an online retailer like Amazon looks at your past history of browsing for a particular product online and then matches this use pattern to effectively target advertisements to you through sites like Facebook and Google so that you are enticed to buy.

This is simple enough, but a similar method sits behind more advanced uses of AI such as self-driving vehicles. Human beings pore over hundreds of thousands of hours of video, labelling every small detail, including road signs, traffic lights, distances from other traffic and so on so that these otherwise random data elements are now labelled accurately for the AI software in self-driving cars to analyse—and then act on.

Some AI is now actually smart enough to write improvements to its own software code as its 'understanding' of the data fed to it increases, suggesting that machines can now 'think' for themselves. There has been astonishment, as I have written here before, at the discovery that these black boxes can autonomously develop the capacity to obfuscate the truth.

But all this is still software. The relentless march of Moore's law: the explosion in computing performance with the attendant reduction in the cost of computing, along with the Internet, which has produced an explosion of data, has allowed the decades-old AI software research ideas of neural networks and machine learning to see the light of day.

It seems that AI is now shifting into the hardware realm, specifically in the development of integrated circuits (ICs). Of the three mainstream hardware platforms—Intel and other CPU chips popular in laptops and servers, ARM chips in mobile devices, and high-performance gaming chips called GPUs, mostly from Nvidia—GPUs seem to have the edge today in AI development. This is because today's CPUs are primarily scalar-based, wherein a single instruction operates on a single piece of data, and GPUs are vector-based, wherein a single instruction operates on a 'linear array' of data called vectors, and Nvidia has capitalized on the opportunity.

There are also a number of chip design start-ups, especially in parts of the world where deep pockets can fund this kind of long gestation period research. For instance, a deep technology start-up called AlphaICs, who are trying to revolutionize the design of ICs to meet AI's future needs. AlphaICs claims to have built a custom hardware platform for 'supervised' self-learning agents that are delivering 'reinforcement' learning today and will provide the foundation for unsupervised learning in the future as AI evolves, in a process they call 'Real AI'.

The AlphaICs Real AI Processor (called RAP™), is based on 'agents', a group of interconnected 'tensors' (mathematical objects analogous to but more general than the vectors I have referenced above that are found in GPUs). Today's GPUs do not have the architecture to handle a divergence of threads needed for reinforcement learning, while agents do.

AlphaICs has also developed a new specialized set of instructions called SIMA™ (Single Instruction Multiple Agents) to increase the energy efficiency of chips. SIMA™ enables multiple agents working asynchronously in groups, in different environments, such as mobile, data centres and PCs, to bring a large level of parallelism at the agent level, thereby significantly increasing the rate of AI learning.

* * *

The application of technology can occur in a variety of fields. Consider this example of how algorithms in conjunction with Phage therapy can help deal with superbugs. Superbugs are bacteria that have become immune to existing antibiotics. The over-prescription of antibiotics and their wide use in poultry, fish and meat farms means that bacteria have had a chance to mutate and become resistant to many antibiotics. To add to this, we are using old ammunition. The last useful class of antibiotics now in use, fluoroquinolone, was discovered in 1962, about sixty years ago.

Antibiotic cocktails that are used to treat superbugs do exist. They are used sparingly and only as a last resort. The irony here is that whether the patient lives or dies, he or she will not end up being a repeat user. As a result, drug companies pour very little of their resources into the discovery of such drugs, as the economic returns from finding a super class of antibiotics simply do not outweigh the costs. Meanwhile, estimates put the number of deaths because of superbugs at more than one million a year, which is likely to grow to 10 million by 2050. That is one death every three seconds. It's time for action, but if big pharma stays away, this action will lie in the realm of start-ups.

Many start-ups are using the explosion in big data and computing power to run complicated algorithms that may eventually provide a breakthrough. The use of big data by start-ups dealing with this problem can broadly be classified into three types. The first lies in the simple but effective mapping of disease patterns within a geography and various sets of people among its population. The second is the use of computational algorithms to presage a scientific molecular-level discovery, which is what most new superbug antibiotic development start-ups are attempting. They use these algorithms in their quest to design a chemistry-based solution that will allow for the isolation of certain proteins in the bacterium, which, when disintegrated by a chemical substance, will kill the bacterium. The third technique is to use genomics, which studies how harmful bacteria have changed in response to antibiotic use, and use this new-found knowledge to arrive at changes in genomic sequencing to kill the resistant bacteria.

However, the fight against superbugs can't be won by IT alone. I recently met Dr Steffanie Strathdee, a chaired professor at the department of medicine at the University of California in San Diego (UCSD). Strathdee is an expert on global health and, apart from her name-endowed professorship at UCSD, is also the associate dean of its department of medicine. Strathdee recounted an intensely personal experience with superbugs, which caused her to start a new line of research. Her husband had been slipping in and out of a coma for two months brought on by a superbug and the doctors had said there was nothing they could do.

Strathdee reached back to her early college training where she had learnt about phages or viruses that attack and kill bacterial cells, a process called phage therapy. Phages were discovered more than 100 years ago by a French–Canadian microbiologist Félix d'Herelle.

There are trillions of phages on the planet that have evolved over millennia to become the perfect predators of bacteria. The phage latches on to and enters the bacterium, and once that is done, proceeds to take over its machinery and turn it into a kind of phage-manufacturing plant. The newly-minted phages then burst out and the bacterial cell dies. To work, phages have to be matched to the bacterial infection.

Strathdee decided to ask for help, which was forthcoming from labs in Russia, the US Navy, Switzerland and even India, among others, and sourced viruses of eight different strains that were known to be phages of Acinetobacter baumannii, nicknamed Iraqibacter. She then injected billions of these phages into her husband Tom Patterson, another scientist at UCSD. Patterson recovered as a result of her last-ditch effort.

Strathdee says that what is needed now are clinical trials to see if this line of therapy works on a broader scale. Strathdee says if she can use this method for one man, then why not for the entire planet? She hopes to create a library of phages or a giant phage bank with specific phage cocktails for many mutations of superbugs. She is on a quest to raise funding to do so.

* * *

The possibilities of the future are based on how tech can be applied to the real world. Technology only matters when it can bring real change to the real world. Innovation requires one to understand this relationship between the digital and the physical.

I have polled senior executives at IT service providers to understand how each sees the digital future. They each have slightly varying views, but all have a strong definition of how and where they want to play in the future, which is heartening, given that there is much fretting among external observers that the future is murky for IT services firms. In addition to chronicling their views, I will highlight examples of work already completed for each firm's clients to envision, design and finally deliver solutions that fit the new direction that technology is now going.

One of the executives I have spoken with is Sanjay Jalona, chief executive officer of Larsen & Toubro Infotech (LTI). I first met Jalona around eighteen years ago when he was the delivery leader for Infosys, charged with that firm's performance on one of Indian IT's first mega deals. The client on this transaction was ABN Amro Bank NV. The global Dutch-heritage bank had retained my then employer TPI to advise on the deal, and as the lead negotiation adviser to the client, I sat across the table from Jalona, his bosses and his teammates who went on to win a large proportion of that transaction. While Jalona was a junior and played a small role in that transaction while taking direction from others, he subsequently climbed the ladder at Infosys. He was eventually recruited to spearhead LTI's evolution from being a privately held subsidiary of Larsen & Toubro Ltd (L&T) into a separate, publicly traded company.

Jalona doesn't like the term 'digital'. In typical marketing speak, which one would expect from an IT services outsourcer, he would rather use the term 'exponential technologies' to define this new world, and by this he means a raft of advancements in technology: 3D printing, virtual reality, face recognition software, artificial intelligence, automated data analytics and so on. His view is that these technologies govern about 20 per cent of the IT spend at end-clients in today's world, but that it is growing at speed—he expects that these technologies will constitute over 80 per cent of the spend by the year 2025.

He is perplexed that while people talk incessantly about a digital world, they seem to forget that the physical world will never go away. So rather than focus solely on digital, he would prefer that the industry focus on the meeting point of the physical and digital worlds, which is where he feels the real value will be delivered, in places such as manufacturing shop floors, airports and oil fields. This focus on the physical aspect is unsurprising, given LTI's long gestation period within L&T.

This marriage of the digital and the physical is apparent in one of the examples Jalona provided. His firm has worked with an oil field firm to automate a large part of the repair and maintenance process of oil extraction machinery that is an integral part of keeping an oil field at peak production efficiency. Many critical pieces of machinery at these oil fields fail with alarming regularity, necessitating service on a regular basis. Jalona says his team worked with the client to put in place an Internet of Things (IoT) solution by building in sensors, beacons and other parts of electronic componentry into these pieces of machinery that could predict a critical machine failure before it occurred. The information exhaust produced by the data that this IoT solution provided also allowed for LTI to accurately predict which spare parts were most needed for the repair of these critical machines, and to instruct its client's logistics systems to place an appropriate quantity of the right spare parts in supply dumps closest to the oil fields, thereby reducing turn-around delays on repairs caused by a shortage of the right spare parts.

One of the main reasons why breakthroughs in computer theory and science such as AI or IoT didn't see the light of day decades ago was simply because both the computing and telecommunications and technology infrastructure available at the time was unequal to the task. In many ways, Xerox delivered several technologies to the world decades ahead of time: the mouse, windows, the facsimile machine, the laser printer and collaborative computing, but failed to capitalize on them.

Today's world is different. As Jalona says, 'If you can imagine something, there is almost certainly a technology already available that can do it.' The art of the possible now lies in obtaining and then orchestrating that technology solution so that it can translate the imagination into reality.

Another example was LTI's work with India's Central Board of Direct Taxes (CBDT). LTI claims to be the primary partner for CBDT's outcome-based programme called Project Insight, which is one of the largest digital transformation initiatives in the country, and which provides comprehensive big data analytics and surveillance solutions.

If someone is paying no tax but is meanwhile posting pictures on Facebook of serial trips to Paris for shopping splurges, something is probably amiss, and the CBDT might want to know more. As I heard a wag once say about social media, 'What (George) Orwell failed to predict was that we would buy the cameras ourselves and our biggest fear was that nobody would be watching.' It appears that the wag was wrong, and that Orwell was right after all.

* * *

The application of current technology can be reconsidered and applied in novel, new ways—such as how AI is applied to tech crowdsourcing. Much of today's software product and hardware infrastructure is delivered through 'as-a-service' model. As-a-service just means the ability to rent and pay for software and hardware as and when it is used, rather than buying an expensive license or powerful computers. Software behemoths such as Oracle and SAP have been pivoting to this model, as have cloud computing infrastructure platforms such as Amazon Web Services (AWS) and Microsoft's Azure.

The rent-versus-own decision ebbs and flows over time. Not so long ago, before India's mobile phone revolution, the country was dotted with ISD/STD call booths in a classic example of as-a-service delivery. You didn't need to own a landline phone when you could simply walk up to a booth and, for a fee, use someone else's phone for a short while. Once it became cheap enough to acquire and use a mobile phone to make calls on one's own, these booths disappeared.

Classical economic thinking would predict that this sort of 'rental' model will not work for cutting-edge software application development, which fundamentally alters the workings of a firm. Firms in the quest for digital disruption will be looking to keep their competition out, and so would prefer to have their own in-house development rather than renting it. This is especially true of start-up firms in the technology space.

While talent is global, opportunity is not. Hiring top engineers locally in Silicon Valley is costly, and not scalable. In addition, employee retention data paints a bleak picture. The average Silicon Valley engineer retains in his or her job for thirteen months. When the time to hire, on-board and handoff are accounted for, employers only get about nine months of productive work from each engineer.

Turing wants to help start-ups hire pre-vetted, high-quality engineers sourced from the global talent pool. The vetting is done using automation and AI. Turing claims that its platform helps developers from all over the world by offering them an opportunity to participate in Silicon Valley and allows start-ups in the valley a fighting chance of being able to access and retain top-quality talent. Turing claims that its customers can just push a button and hire exceptional pre-vetted remote software engineers on demand.

In this age of open-source programming and the ready availability of free programming libraries with a simple click of the cursor, start-ups and corporations are increasingly open to the idea of turning to the programming community at large, in a phenomenon called 'crowdsourcing'. IT services firms are certainly wise to this phenomenon; Wipro already owns Topcoder, the world's largest platform-based crowdsourcing service. Turing uses ongoing testing of its contractors' work performance in order to continue to provide only top-quality talent and eschews dependence on what the programmer's resume says.

* * *

The application of technology to solve problems in the real world may not always work and, in fact, may even worsen the problems in an already flawed system. To aid college applications to UK universities in normal times, teachers at British schools issue 'predictive' grades to students who are about to take their public A-level (class 12) examinations. Apart from a student's extracurricular performance, predictive grades are used as one of the main factors by universities in the UK to base their admission decisions for incoming bachelor's degree students. These admissions are granted on a conditional basis, which means universities base their final decisions on the actual scores achieved on public competitive exams that are released just before universities begin their autumn terms.

Given the COVID-19 pandemic, the British government directed its Office of Qualifications and Examinations Regulation, or Ofqual, to find an alternative to these school-leaving qualifications. Earlier studies by Ofqual had established that teachers' predictive scores could be biased by gender, ethnicity and age. To move away from such biases, Ofqual decided to use an algorithm to stand in for 2020's cancelled public examinations.

That algorithm should ideally have had two goals. One, to ensure fairness and avoid grade inflation; and two, to ensure that students get assessed as accurately as possible for university admissions. Under government directives, however, Ofqual ended up focusing on just the first goal.

This itself should have sounded a warning bell, given that moving away from teachers' predictive scores would necessarily entail arbitrary standardization constraints that would be applied to the algorithm. And sure enough, arbitrary conditions were used. For instance, the algorithm corrected not only for a student's grade, but also for the average performance of the student's school, done basically by choosing a standardized model that would predict a distribution for 2020 exam scores and match it with the distribution for 2019. This relentless 'pursuit of the mean' simply meant that a student's score could be ratcheted way down based on how his or her seniors in school had performed the year before, and would not be based on his or her individual performance.

If a system is flawed to begin with, trying to fix its flaws with a ham-handed approach like regressing everyone to a mythical mean is only going to make matters worse. Had the second objective of accurately assessing a student's performance been paramount, it is likely that Ofqual would have found a more nuanced answer to the problem by adopting both qualitative and quantitative methods. This too would have had its share of problems but would almost certainly not have affected as many as 40 per cent of students.

Organizations the world over are beginning to find that applying over-simplistic AI algorithms to what are highly nuanced and complex problems doesn't work. Many of these problems are beyond the realm of data science, and we must accept that it will be years before AI algorithms are refined enough to be used as a cure-all for all that ails the world.

* * *

But with any development of technology comes an issue of ethics. There is a philosophical question that must be pondered by anyone who attempts to tamper with the human body through experimental technology. Electronic implants that push the frontiers of medicine, when used to achieve ends such as restoring eyesight, are indeed inspiring. Meanwhile, science-based attempts at using the gene-editing tool 'CRISPR', short for 'clusters of regularly interspaced short palindromic repeats', to achieve similar ends are also laudable. At its most basic level, CRISPR is a tool for gene editing that has immense potential for precise and efficient modifications. It has been used to treat genetic diseases and genetically modify plants. However, many scientists consider it unethical to try manipulating genes or implanting electronics in the human body simply to boost the performance of otherwise healthy people.

There is now word that China has been conducting trials to produce bio-hacked enhanced soldiers. John Ratcliffe, US director of national intelligence, made this claim in a *Wall Street Journal* op-ed.

'There are no ethical boundaries to Beijing's pursuit of power,' wrote Ratcliffe. 'U.S. intelligence shows that China has conducted "human testing" on members of the People's Liberation Army (PLA) in hope of developing soldiers with "biologically enhanced capabilities".' Apart from the startling op-ed by Ratcliffe, other studies have also suggested that China, unlike the West, has pushed the ethical boundaries of cyborg experimentation well beyond what would generally be acceptable in most of the world. (A cyborg is a human being on whom many organs, limbs and other parts have been replaced by mechanical or computerized structures.)

According to a paper by the Jamestown Foundation, 'China's Military Biotech Frontier: CRISPR, Military-Civil Fusion, and the New Revolution in Military Affairs', Chinese scientists across academic institutions and commercial enterprises have been at the forefront of experimentation with this technique from the start, including the company BGI (formerly Beijing Genomics Inc.), which also manages China's National Gene Bank. China's CRISPR work has rapidly progressed into clinical trials that involve the application of these gene editing techniques to animals and humans. This may be because some of the regulatory requirements for medical research in China are less strict and demanding. For instance, there are currently at least fourteen trials of CRISPR underway across Chinese hospitals that are primarily exploring its potential to treat cancer. Strikingly, medical institutions run by the PLA, particularly the PLA General Hospital and the Academy of Military Medical Sciences, are involved in five of the trials known to be underway at present.

To me, the dark side of bio-hacking represents a clear and present threat, more significant than the potentially unethical uses of AI. At least the dangers of personal data used by AI are already regulated or getting regulated in most of the world. Bio-hacking is less well understood, and its regulation, let alone international treaties against its misuse, seems nowhere on the horizon. That's unfortunate.

In addition to bio-experimentation, the ethicality of other technology development processes should be an important consideration with regard to whether the ends justify the means. Using prisoners for AI is like a double-forked process, like what was done in a 2019 experiment with Finnish prisoners. Besides skilling them, it could also lead to exploitation. It appears that governments across the world are confused, even schizophrenic, about how they deal with advances in AI and the human costs they may cause through loss of employment.

Under a Universal Basic Income or UBI programme, all citizens get paid a basic wage whether or not they are employed. Many UBI proponents, including AI entrepreneurs such as Elon Musk and Mark Zuckerberg, have said that they see UBI as the only solution to the problem of mass unemployment caused by AI and other advances in information technology.

The basic premise behind UBI is not unlike the premise behind universal healthcare coverage systems. Northern European welfare states have grappled with such issues for decades. They have outrageously high rates of taxation, but, relative to other nations at least, a semi-efficient way to plough these taxes back into welfare schemes for their citizens.

Finland first began experimenting with the concept of UBI in January 2017. The pilot programme allowed 2000 unemployed Finns to receive a UBI dole, even when they tried out casual employment at odd jobs. These 2000 were to be compared against a control group of 1,37,000 employed Finns to allow the government to draw a conclusion on UBI's efficacy.

There are two problems with every dole, however. One, it must be paid for by all citizens, which means higher taxes, and two, doles act as a disincentive for recipients who would otherwise be forced to go out and find paying work.

In 2019, Finnish prison labour was used to feed AI. To throw light on this, I first need to explain one of the things that makes AI useful for applications such as driverless cars: inexpensive labour in countries such as India and Sri Lanka, where employees spend hours on end categorizing and labelling data elements so that they make sense to an AI program.

Finland decided to turn to a source of inexpensive labour, its prison inmates, to categorize and label these data elements. The Verge (a media website) reported that inmates at two prisons in Finland are performing a new type of labour: classifying data to train AI algorithms for a start-up. While the start-up in question, Vainu, sees the partnership as a kind of prison reform that teaches valuable skills, other experts say it plays into the exploitation of prisoners being required to work for very low wages. Vainu has been using Finnish prisoners for this work for some time; news reports at the end of 2020 indicated that Vainu was continuing its work at Finnish prisons.

Vainu found cheap labour by enlisting the Finnish Criminal Sanctions Agency (CSA), which had access to more Finnish-speaking labour than Mechanical Turk, according to *The Verge*. Vainu is now having its work done at two Finnish prisons, one in Helsinki and the other in Turku. In turn, Vainu paid the CSA roughly the equivalent of what it would have paid on Mechanical Turk. The Vainu team hopes to expand elsewhere in Finland and other countries where it can be hard to find people willing to do this type of work in local languages.

Mechanical Turk is itself no great paymaster. Research by Kotaro Hara, a professor at Singapore Management University, and his collaborators reveals that the median wage of a worker at Turk is around $2 an hour. Compare this to the US minimum wage of $7.25 an hour, and the savings become readily apparent.

The philosophical and ethical questions that this precedent of using prison labour brings to light are beyond the scope of this book. Suffice to say that if feeding AI algorithms is already exploitative, one shudders to think how much more exploitative the algorithms would be once finally in place.

* * *

New technology can amplify the effect of social and cultural biases. This can help us uncover and understand such biases. As a result, new systems are necessary to help prevent any disastrous consequences that can result from this amplification.

Kenneth Arrow was a British-born American mathematician and was once the youngest Nobel laureate ever. In his doctoral thesis, completed in the 1950s, Arrow identified that in any electoral system where three or more preferences exist, the proponents of the minority voice paradoxically have the ability to dictate the broader choice—in a finding now called Arrow's Paradox. Arrow's Paradox can cause an election which should have a predictable outcome to become a farce since the outcome can be gamed to allow minority factions to prevail.

This can be illustrated with an example: Let's say a population has three preferences in the run-up to an election which pits binary choices against each other—A: go to war or B: don't go to war. While there are only two choices (A or B), the voting populace itself may be distributed along three lines as follows: one, the hawks—who are in a minority but absolutely want to go to war, and two, others who form the majority of voters but are roughly equally split—the doves who prefer not to go to war under any circumstance, and the realists who don't want to go to war unless it's absolutely necessary. In an election where only two choices can be made, the minority hawks, who want to go to war immediately, have the ability to dictate the outcome by convincing the realists who believe in not going to war unless really necessary by prevailing on the realists that war is actually needed. This isn't the minority swing vote we are normally told about—it's a systematic way for a minority going about setting a voting agenda such that it carries the day.

Countless elections the world over have shown how Arrow's mathematics work in actual practice. One example was in Italy, where a young lawyer with no political experience was asked to form the government, and in countless state elections in India. How then, do individual members of the electorate, who might actually represent the majority opinion, get their voices heard by those from the minority who, thanks to Arrow's Paradox, may now be in power?

While faced with news like compliance with data privacy and the like, we worry about our privacy online. While that is natural, when the opposite is the case and we want our voices heard, we do not really know how to speak up in the electronic age. We need a new method to allow people's voices to be heard without going through today's social media tools such as Twitter and Facebook, which are fraught with legal challenges, regulatory problems, and investigations.

Starbucks, and others like it, often have a large workforce, many of whom don't have email addresses at the firm and cannot communicate with the senior management. Conversely, these employers sometimes need to reach out to their workforce in an efficient way. Starbucks had a fiasco some years ago when it was put into the spotlight for racist behaviour at its cafés. The CEO reacted immediately by closing all US cafés for a day to train employees on removing racial biases.

Another example of where such platforms could be of use when workers need to organize—or when corporations need to get the word out to workers, would be with firms such as Uber and Ola, who have large 'casual' workforces who do not always have a sufficient voice. The average voter at least has an election every few years; it is doubtful whether such direct mechanisms exist at corporations that have an 'independent' workforce.

After all, as a Washington lawyer once told me, the three rules for people in power are: deny everything, concede nothing—and if caught out, allege fraud.

Chapter 14

Musings for the Leader

Given the ubiquitous nature of technology in today's world, it has become imperative upon leaders in the tech world to make decisions not only from the profit-minded perspective but also the welfare of the general public. Take, for example, the issue of data privacy.

The laissez-faire approach to data privacy has allowed the growth of business models based on attention capture, surveillance and user opinion modification. Indifference for the past two and a half decades to what happens on the Internet has destabilized political systems, even allowing for foreign interference in American elections.

If tech laissez-faire has run its course, what are the alternatives? The first is to ape China and impose net nationalism, which makes the state the predominant authority over all things online. This will inexorably lead to the global Internet splitting up into several national ones. The clear and present danger is that such national Internets can become instruments of state power. They might end up serving as a means of disseminating state propaganda, monitoring dissent and furthering crony capitalism.

Tech-nationalism is not the only alternative, though. We also have democracy, which holds that matters of public importance should be decided by the people—and that people should control the excesses of both private and government power. We have laws against child labour, for instance, and against the excessive use of force by police authorities. Similarly, when it comes to the Internet, democratic principles hold that legitimate governments can make rules so long as these serve the interests of the people.

This is the concept of tech democracy. The only justifications for any non-democratic intervention would include national security, the defence of institutions, the preservation of markets, the need for retaliation against a belligerent foreign power, and so on. But it is the interests of the public and not the whims of a leader, nor the interests of corporations, that should guide us. Getting the tech policy balance right is a key challenge for democratic governments around the world.

As technology becomes more ubiquitous, the more the world will have to comprehend and analyse its effect on society. This would necessarily mean that technology will become part of the political debates in governments across the world. Being a leader means that one would need to stay conscious and proactive with regard to how people use technology and how to manage the ill-effects it can have.

In late 2018, I wrote in a column in *Mint* of the hearings at which Sundar Pichai, Google's chief executive officer, was grilled by members of the US Congress. In that column, I also wrote about the rise of anti-big-tech activism from many new quarters, one of them being the Trojan Horse of self-righteous employees within big tech itself.

This led to an exchange with Paul Schmidt, an old friend, who was once a 'top gun' F-15 fighter pilot in the US Air Force and is now a renowned technology consultant. Schmidt had read my column and remarked that the white-collar social activists I spoke of have themselves contributed to what he calls the 'big tech devastation' of the cities they inhabit. He pointed to San Francisco and Seattle, both once beautiful cities that are now overrun with homelessness and unlivable downtown conditions. Big tech's overpaid employees have led a bidding war to drive up housing prices in these cities and have contributed in other ways to edging out non-tech employment, except for the food delivery runners, taxi drivers and office cleaning personnel who linger on to serve their techie masters. In my own experience, while in downtown San Francisco in 2018, it seemed to me that anybody outside this circle of the served and their servers appears to be either homeless or hopelessly addicted to drugs; sometimes both.

As an aside, my thoughts turned to Bengaluru and other Indian cities that have suffered as a result of the earlier tech boom in outsourced services, though not in quite the same way as San Francisco and Seattle. In a column in *Mint*, I had pointed out that outsourcing tech companies that have operations in Indian cities have to bear a lot of the blame—and pay the costs—for restoring some semblance of liveability to these cities, rather than conveniently placing the blame solely at the government's doorstep.

Given the decline in cities such as San Francisco and Seattle, Schmidt finds it hypocritical that big tech employees are turning 'activist'. He notes that while big tech is happy to experiment with building a censored search engine for China or to place private data there to track 'internal enemies', it is against doing anything to help its own government in the US in attempts to curtail its reach through legislation.

Unfortunately, the Silicon Valley bubble is getting a big dose of the real world, or at least a dose of another bubble that has long been existent outside the valley. This is the bubble that in Europe, resides in Brussels, and in the US, resides inside the Beltway or the ring road that encircles Washington, D.C. One bubble is a tech echo-chamber, and the others are political echo-chambers. Now that these bubbles are colliding, they find that they are not very compatible. What makes this clash of bubbles monumental is that some big tech firms have the clout of a medium-sized country and revenues that exceed the gross domestic product (GDP) of many.

A moment's reflection shows that 2018 was the year when the governmental comeuppance for big tech started. Facebook has faced a string of woes, which started with the Cambridge Analytica scandal. Later, two more problems hit the beleaguered social media giant. One was a reported breach of personal data from millions of its user accounts, soon followed by an exposé in the *New York Times*, which evidently showed that Facebook had been continuing to provide sensitive personal data from its users to other big tech firms. This, despite its apologies over the Cambridge Analytica affair and hand-on-heart promise to never let it happen again. As far as Google is concerned, Pichai's appearance in December 2018 in front of the US Congress is just the beginning of that government's efforts to rein in the tech giant.

During 2018, the bubble of tech had been colliding with other governmental bubbles too. The Europeans passed their General Data Protection Regulations and put them into effect that year, handing back the ownership rights over personal data to the individual. This shift has caused much friction in the tech world, with the real threat of billions of dollars in fines being imposed on big tech firms for flouting these norms.

In India, Facebook-owned WhatsApp is coming under increasing pressure from the government to step up and take more accountability for the spread of false news that has sometimes led to violence. The government believes, rightly, that the veil of user privacy should be lifted, and people who encourage violence by propagating doctored videos of horrendous events that have occurred elsewhere in the world and labelling them as Indian should be caught and prosecuted. Recent news has Twitter running afoul of India's new IT Rules that came into effect on 26 May 2021. Twitter has appointed a local chief in India to deal with specific issues that arise in this country.

Like the Roman god Janus, after whom January is named, big tech is two-faced; when asked for transparency from governments, it cries 'user privacy', but is willing to compromise that same privacy when revenue is involved, whether by entering China or giving data to other firms. One hopes that the world will settle on how to bring rationality in regulating big tech the world over.

* * *

Being at the forefront of tech development requires a responsibility for the welfare of society at large. This means that one requires a good understanding of the implications of tech use on a wider scale than simply profit. One needs to be aware of how stupidity with technology can derail true social and cultural growth.

Almost all AI computer program development seems to be 'top down', which looks at the thinking and reasoning accomplished by the more advanced areas of our brain. It is not 'bottom up' and so does not start with the deeply embedded thought patterns that have established themselves in our brains long before we evolved into Homo sapiens. In March 2018, Umair Haque, in a blog post titled 'The Age of the Imbecile' on the website medium.com, defined our current age as 'catastrophically stupid'.

Haque's piece is wide ranging; it touches on several socio-economic and political issues and scolds the reader by saying that it is we, the individuals, who the world over have actually chosen all this, and have made our present world one of 'futility, emptiness, and hollowness'. Haque traces at least a portion of the explosion of stupidity to the last financial crisis in 2008. He points out five different types of what he calls imbecilic thought that have produced our current age.

The first is economic stupidity—as evidenced by nationalism, populism and austerity programmes. The second is social stupidity, which is the idea that society can function without a well-defined set of social contracts, which allows for an 'Uber that replaces ambulances' and 'hyperloops that replace buses'. The third, and the subject for more exploration here, is the idea of 'tech-determinism', which holds that technology has the ability to solve all our problems. The fourth form of Haque's definition of stupidity is 'cultural stupidity' that gives rise to extremist religion and racism. Haque's fifth and final type of stupidity is psychological—evidenced by our denial or self-chosen ignorance, where we simply go on with our lives thinking that everything will be okay and go back to normal.

The tech-determinism that Haque speaks of was of special interest to me. I think this form of catastrophic stupidity is reflected in the attitude of the modern individual who experiences the forefront of technological change. I find it curious that people find it acceptable that their email or messaging provider has the ability to peruse the contents of their emails and messages and suggest appropriate responses. In the old days, this would be no different than having the postman or the courier company steam open envelopes and read sensitive mail addressed only to you. In the physical world, this is frowned upon, if not an actual crime. In the tech-world, we accept it as normal.

Yet, many people I speak to seem to be able to accept this technological development nonchalantly, naively believing that this makes their lives easier. The same extends to our willingness to cough up our Aadhaar numbers to firms that ask, and our fingerprints, facial images and detailed medical records to firms that don't always actually ask, such as our smartphone manufacturers or social networking sites or medical insurers. All this for an imagined increase in 'productivity' and 'convenience'.

* * *

Another example of understanding the implications of technology in society is the issue of misinformation on the Internet. One would have thought that democratic access to a large variety of news from all corners of the globe would have opened up the echo chambers in towns and rural areas, but the hard fact is that the Internet has pulled the other way. There are far fewer news outlets now than there were some years ago. The travesty is that many of these organizations are not news outlets; they are social networks such as Facebook, WhatsApp and Twitter. These have no journalistic norms. Anyone can say anything at any time about any topic with scant respect for the truth. Everything is an opinion, but not clearly labelled as such. As a result, much of the 'news' available on these platforms is biased. The unscrupulous sale of personal information and meddling by inimical foreign regimes can potentially even influence the outcome of an election. Worse, the spread of false and malicious news can stoke violence at short notice. We have already seen this in India, when WhatsApp came under Indian regulatory scrutiny after a doctored video that originated as an innocent advertisement in Pakistan spread on that medium and stoked violence.

Most Americans now get their news from dubious Internet sources. The hardening of political stances on both sides of the divide is plain to see, and the acute polarization of the average American's viewpoint is painful to watch. For India, the danger is that, like the US, such extreme polarization can happen in a few short years. Also, the echo chamber has been greatly enhanced by the highly targeted algorithms that these companies use. The algorithms were built around making users stay online longer and click through to advertisements. They are likely to bombard users with information that serves to reinforce what the algorithm thinks the searcher needs to know. For instance, if I search for a particular type of phone on an e-commerce site even once, future searches are likely to autocomplete that search by showing that phone when I next open the app. It is the same with news. If I show a preference for right-wing leaning posts, for instance, the algorithms are likely to provide me with ever more right-wing posts from people and organizations. As they familiarize themselves with the Internet, newly online Indians are bound to fall prey to the echo chamber algorithms that social network firms use, as well as other algorithms that ensure they spend inordinate amounts of time within the bubble of one social network, therefore becoming easy marks for targeted advertising—both for products and of political viewpoints.

Much can be said about how we should approach the impending Internet misinformation storm. I shall attempt to make a beginning here. First, we know that tech firms are already under fire from all quarters. Just as they are struggling to meet calls to contain the online spread of misinformation and hate speech online, they are being accused of suppressing both left-wing and right-wing views. There is no pleasing anyone on this issue. Nonetheless, we need to act. Second, unlike the US, which has now become unlikely to directly regulate such firms, India might need to chart its own path by keeping them under check before they proliferate. In the US, these issues were not sufficiently legislated for and have existed for over a decade. Existing legislation has been tested by the American court system, which has held that companies like Google and Facebook clearly engage in both free speech and press activities when they display content created by third parties. Free speech is inherent in the Constitution of many other democracies, including India's. This means that new Indian legislation needs to preserve free speech while still applying pressure to make sure that Internet content is filtered for accuracy, and sometimes, plain decency. Let us remember that our courts do not legislate; they ensure adherence to existing legislation.

The third issue is corporate responsibility. Facebook, for instance, has started to address this matter by publishing 'transparency reports' and setting up an 'oversight board' to act as a sort of Supreme Court for Facebook's internal matters. However, for all these companies' efforts at transparency, we cannot ignore the fact that these numbers reflect judgements that are made behind closed doors. What should be regulatory attempts to influence the transparency of information that members of the public see are instead being converted into secret corporate processes. We have no way of knowing the extent of biases that may be inherent inside each firm. The fact that their main algorithms target advertising and hyper-personalization of content makes them further suspect as arbiters of balanced news. This means that those who use social media platforms must pull in another direction to maintain access to a range of sources and views. Whether this will be possible as the hinterland of India comes online is doubtful. We need strong intervention. Else, in addition to the media, which has largely been the responsible fourth estate, we may well witness the creation of an unmanageable fifth estate in the form of big tech.

* * *

The vast and seemingly endless potential of technological development means that opinions will vary as to where the world is headed and decisions must be made. But not all decisions could be considered beneficial for the working population. Buzzwords such as robotic process automation (RPA), AI, ML and cloud-based software as a service (SaaS) model of software delivery are prevalent today. They are used by many, but understood by few.

Firms that sell technology are often at fault. They seek to confuse buyers, since this allows them to capitalize on 'information asymmetry', where buyers always know less than sellers. This tactic is especially useful nowadays as technology buyers are afraid of being overtaken by their competitors, or worse yet, 'disrupted' by technology-driven upstarts. It isn't always sellers vs buyers. Even senior executives at technology firms have serious fallouts with their colleagues or bosses because of honest differences of opinion on how the future is likely to pan out. This 'technology dissonance' isn't surprising; these executives are trying to bet the entire futures of their firms on one direction or another.

Thomas Kurian, long a senior leader at Oracle Inc., is now Google Cloud's global boss. He and his twin brother George, CEO of NetApp Inc., were my classmates in high school. The difference between the twins and me then was that they occupied the front benches, while I was a dedicated denizen of the last bench.

The difference now is that they hold positions of power, while I still can only make noise from the back.

Before Kurian left Oracle for Google, he had been placed on 'long leave'. He appears to have been affected by this technology dissonance between executives. Kurian was silent about his leave, while an Oracle spokesperson said he was 'taking some time off' and that she expected him to return soon. Nonetheless, Bloomberg reported that Kurian's leave stemmed from differences with Oracle co-founder Larry Ellison on the software maker's cloud business. According to Bloomberg's report, Kurian evidently wanted to allow Oracle's software to run on the cloud platforms of its competitors Amazon.com Inc. and Microsoft Corp., while Ellison wanted Oracle to run its own cloud infrastructure from which Oracle's products will be made available.

Like Microsoft, Oracle has a huge command over the enterprise computing space, and so the shift to a cloud-based SaaS delivery model should, in theory, have been easy to accomplish. Bloomberg says Oracle's cloud offering has not been able to gain traction in its battle with Amazon Web Services and Microsoft's Azure platform.

While we are on the subject of technology dissonance, I must also touch upon rpa2ai. Its CEO, Kashyap Kompella, was a colleague of mine in the mid-2000s. Robotic Process Automation or RPA and AI talent is scarce even inside the industry for those who are actually building solutions, let alone among non-technical investors and acquirers. The firm has tried to provide unbiased research about these areas to its clients, often investors who are looking to take bets on RPA and AI start-ups.

A couple of years ago, the firm put out a press release based on its research. In sum, it makes the following observations:

- RPA has greater potential to significantly automate and change the work of millions of white-collar professionals than AI.

- The RPA marketplace is attracting a significant amount of venture capital funding, enterprise attention and employee anxiety.
- While it can be an effective way to improve efficiencies and processes, RPA is regularly mis-sold as ML or AI-enabled. In reality, most RPA products have little to no ML or AI capabilities.
- RPA products vary widely in their provenance, functionality, architecture, deployment options and geographic footprint. One size does not fit all.
- Business buyers are often avoiding and not involving IT departments in their decision-making processes, resulting in failed implementations.

According to Kompella, the RPA market is witnessing hyper-growth and expectations are sky-high. As a result, some degree of disappointment is inevitable, but RPA can change the global services landscape and impact a number of white-collar jobs.

I can attest to having seen this play out in the bids that IT services vendors are making to their clients. Many of these bids promise to reduce human workers and replace them with RPA 'bots', which do office work. Some vendors are also beginning to set expectations with investors by letting them know that while revenue growth may slow down due to less people being billable, margins will likely go up as more processes become automated. Time will tell.

* * *

Understanding the nature of tech evolution is important for leaders to make good decisions. This includes not only how technology is evolving but how humans are evolving alongside their new technology. Cloud computing and as-a-service offerings are causing a fundamental shift in how corporations consume technology solutions. As-a-service means the ability to rent and pay for software and hardware as and when it is used, rather than buying an expensive license or powerful computers. Big tech has responded to this by setting up cloud computing behemoths—Amazon, Google and Microsoft are all deep into this game. They have scaled up into this space from almost nowhere.

The rent-versus-own decision ebbs and flows over time. Classical thinking would predict that this sort of rental model will not work for cutting-edge tech that fundamentally alters the workings of a firm. But the economics, at least for now, sides with the rental model. The models used in cloud services and solutions work on the premise of economies of scale derived from large operations. This means that computing capability is becoming more centralized. But today's buyer behaviour also demands less 'latency'—or quicker response times—for almost all uses. Centralizing services runs counter to latency. The physical distance from a computing device affects response times, even if the network/Internet connection to the centralized computer is on the fattest possible pipe with massive data throughput. That is why broking firms demand real estate space that is close to a stock exchange. They want to set up their computers close to the computer where stocks are traded.

If the Internet of Things is to be useful, IoT devices need to have the ability to communicate with each other over long distances. Many 'connected things' in remote areas are at long distances from the nearest telecommunications station, or deep within buildings that shield them from a wireless signal. Others are on the move—being shipped from the factory to the consumer, for instance—resulting in spotty signal. Until now, machine-to-machine communication has relied on 2G networks, long considered insufficient for human interaction. While this may today be enough for unsophisticated equipment at the perimeter or on the move, the amount of data being communicated from machine to machine is now increasing as products grow in technical sophistication.

While machines at the edge are evolving, humanity also evolves along with the technologies it invents. Humans and tech now overlap so much that we have become one with our inventions. We have now gone beyond the smartphone and its increasing capability to deliver what was yesterday's supercomputer into a miniaturized handheld. The use of wearable devices is popping up everywhere. The healthcare and fitness industries have introduced many promising wearables. Technologies like virtual reality and augmented reality will push this frontier further.

When this latency and communication variable is thrown into the equation, the only way is for enterprises to shift their computing capability closer to the 'edge'. This is the point where it is most needed, whether that point is in an autonomous machine or in the hands of a human. This is where the rubber meets the road. The edge, then, is the new 'point of truth'.

* * *

Capitalism has a reputation for exploiting workers in the sole pursuit of profit. But being a good leader necessarily requires one to understand the situation of the working class; after all, companies are nothing without the workers. When I was entering the corporate world, my father, who was a doctor, gave me a copy of the *Tao Te Ching*, translated by R.L. Wing, called *The Tao of Power*. I was far too young to make any sense of it at the time, but ploughed my way through the tome, understanding very little and retaining even less.

This now yellowing book, which has also taken on that pleasant olfactory character that only old books can, is still on my bookshelf. I pull it down from time to time and read snatches of it—an act which always results in giving me something to ponder upon. Many of the passages have taken on new meaning for me in the decades that have passed since I was first given the book. I pulled it off the shelf again recently and opened it to a page at random. Call it stichomancy if you will, but out popped this passage:

> The Tao in Nature, Reduces the excessive and supplements the insufficient.
> The Tao in Man is not so; He reduces the insufficient,
> Because he serves the excessive.
> Who then can use excess to serve the world?
> Those who possess the Tao (of Nature).
> Therefore, Evolved Individuals, Act without expectation,
> Succeed without taking credit, And have no desire to display their excellence.

Indeed. As Wing (whose identity is shrouded in mystery, but who legend has it, is a woman) points out in her annotations on this passage: 'On the social plateau, individuals who attempt to dominate others trigger a natural psychological response from their society: a collective urge to neutralize the effect of the excessive members.

'The complement of this response, in group psychology, is to direct help toward individuals who have insufficient means. Because evolved individuals understand this pattern of energy in the universe, they are able to use it to protect their position while they bring progress to their world. So that energy will flow in their direction, they reduce their position by maintaining an atmosphere of moderation and humility in their relationships with others. They then use this energy to alter reality through the focus of their attitudes and convictions.'

It appears as if the recent clamour for 'compassionate capitalism' comes from urges such as these, and on the face of it, is rooted in the well-intentioned tendency of people to speak up for justice and equity. But those calling for compassionate capitalism need to be aware that such statements can come off as nugatory or, worse yet, can rebound. Let me explain with a real-life example from the technology industry:

The media was rife with news of Yahoo's shareholders' vote on Thursday, 8 June 2017. Electing to approve Yahoo's sale to Verizon made them richer by billions of dollars, while also enriching Marissa Mayer, then the chief executive officer of Yahoo, by almost $264 million. Considering that Mayer had been at the erstwhile Internet giant for about five years, this would mean that she earned almost $1 million for each week she had been at the company.

One could argue that Mayer's windfall has very little to do with her work at Yahoo, since the firm failed on many fronts when compared to its arch-rival Google, and is instead due to the investment performance of two bets placed years ago by Jerry Yang, one of Yahoo's founders, in two Asian Internet giants—the Alibaba group in China and Yahoo Japan. Nonetheless, Yahoo's stock more than trebled in value during Mayer's tenure, going up from around $16 to about $50 a share on 7 June 2017. And since most of Mayer's pay was in stock and stock options, she stood to benefit handsomely.

My question is this: Who is expected to be compassionate with the thousands of Yahoo staff who lost their jobs during Mayer's watch? Mayer or the shareholders? After all, Mayer was acting to benefit the shareholders of the company, who are the true capitalists. It is they who provided their capital by buying ownership stakes in Yahoo. Mayer is just one of the many lucky managers who have made fortunes simply by sticking around due to the stock option-based compensation structures that are de rigueur in today's corporations, made possible in part by the seminal work linking stock options and executive compensation done at my alma mater, the University of Rochester, by its professors Michael Jensen, William Meckling and Kevin Murphy.

True compassionate capitalism would mean that the shareholders of Yahoo are willing to forgo some of the profits they stand to make from the deal to benefit the axed employees. Mayer was just their agent. And it is so with many Indian technology firms, whether late-stage start-ups or long-established bellwethers, which are now increasingly managed by professionals while the promoter group, or other early investors, have taken a back seat.

If they want to be paragons of compassionate capitalism, the natural next step would be for these investors to share their current dividends and future profits from their stock holdings with the lower-level workers at these firms, who are now presumably cannon fodder in a relentless world which encourages survival of the fittest.

To be fair, it is these very workers who were until recently accustomed to treating their employers shabbily by disloyally changing employers for small raises in remuneration. These workers were just as much 'capitalists' who chose to maximize their returns. Capitalism, like loyalty, is a reciprocal arrangement.

I would advise caution before we use terms like compassionate capitalism. The natural curveball effect of terms such as these mean they will come back home to roost. For after all, as Lao Tzu says, 'What is curved becomes whole.'

Chapter 15

Musings for the Empath—as Experience Designer, Caregiver and Storyteller

The effect of widespread technology use goes underinvestigated due to the perceived advantages that new technology affords us in modern life. For every positive change in social and cultural life, there is a negative that can make things much worse if gone unnoticed. The rise of social media is one such example. During the 1980s, the penultimate decade of US newspaper ascendancy, hundreds of news organizations existed to serve the country, as they still do in multilingual India. The rise of social media put paid to that. One would have thought that democratic access would have opened up to a large variety of news from all corners of the globe, but the hard fact is that the Internet has pulled the other way. There are far fewer news outlets now than there were some years ago.

The problem is that social networks don't have journalistic norms. Anyone can say anything on any topic. Almost everything is an opinion but not clearly labelled as such. As a result, much of the 'news' available on these platforms is biased. Also, the spread of false and malicious news at warp speed can stoke violence. As I pointed out in the previous chapter, we have already seen this in India, when WhatsApp came under scrutiny after a doctored video that originated as an innocuous advertisement in Pakistan spread and stoked violence.

'Wild West' attitudes have since calmed down slightly, thanks to fact-check revelations by real journalists and pressure from politicians the world over. Under America's 1996 Communications Decency Act, online platforms have the power (and immunity) to block posts that they deem lewd, excessively violent, inimical to others' interests and so on, even if the post is otherwise protected under US free speech laws.

Politicians from both sides of the divide are showing a willingness to externally police and monitor social networks, rather than leave the job to these platforms. Former US President Donald Trump asked for Section 230 to be repealed in a tweeted response to Facebook's decision to take down unverified claims of corruption by Biden's family. Adding fuel to this fire, in 2020, associate justice Clarence Thomas of the US Supreme Court referenced the whole of Section 230 in a decision on another matter that had relied on a rare interpretation of it to deny immunity in Malwarebytes Inc. vs Enigma Software Group USA, LLC. Associate justice Thomas agreed with a judicial decision taken to turn down an appeal on the case, which had been decided in a lower court, but in his written opinion, he launched into a musing on Section 230 in general, arguing that US courts had interpreted it too broadly. In his view, its provisions had been used by US companies to censor free speech beyond the original intent of the law.

While this may seem like an obscure US ruling that has no locus standi elsewhere, America's experience in recent years with the Internet should serve as a warning to the world. The hardening of stances on both sides of the political aisle and the acute polarization of views are painful to watch. The proximate cause is social media. India, where these platforms are also quite pervasive, faces similar troubles.

* * *

The manner in which certain technologies are used in modern culture is very relevant to understanding how these technologies actually affect people. When it comes to social media, most millennials, my children included, grew up with the Internet all around them. Millennials have a powerful understanding of how social media works. My speculation is that it is the millennials' mode of thinking and segmenting people on social media that was used by Cambridge Analytica when that firm sought to use Facebook data to influence various plebiscites.

My son has been trying to build a start-up that will allow celebrities to easily interact with their fans via a take-off on a type of social-media app. One rule for how social media works is called the '1-9-90' rule. Only 1 per cent of those on social media are 'influencers' who actively create content. 9 per cent are 'advocates'—that is, the ones who comment and add their own perspective to the content put out by the 1 per cent. The rest—that is, the 90 per cent—stay silent, simply consuming what the 1 per cent and its 9 per cent following churns out. These 'enthusiasts' constitute 90 per cent of those on social media. Most fall into this category because the beauty of social media is to discover what's out there, not necessarily campaign for it like advocates do.

Grabbing the attention of the 1 per cent is key, but since many of these posters are celebrities, this is unlikely to happen without significant expense. If that's the case, what is the alternative? It is the advocates or the 9 per cent. So, it is the mouthy middle advocates who will give someone who wants domination over social media the most bang for the buck.

This is a critical insight. Getting an influencer to plug your brand, while ideal, is likely difficult. That is not to say that one shies away from this community, just that one recognizes that the cost/value tradeoff may not be as attractive as targeting the advocates. The key lies in creating a conversation to engage these advocates to get their attention. If your brand or message is top of mind for the advocates, your message can be effectively sent across to the enthusiasts—or the 90 per cent. So, one should selectively use tactics to stoke this mouthy middle to react. In politics, for example, this might mean circulating incendiary content that makes this advocate class react.

Review websites like Glassdoor, Yelp, or even Amazon's reviews pages are prime examples of influencers, advocates and enthusiasts, and each of us falls into one of these three segments at one point or another. An influencer creates the store, the product or the restaurant. An advocate would have purchased the product, eaten at the restaurant or bought some type of clothing at the store. Whether they enjoyed the product or not is beside the point, but it is the fact that advocates will comment on or review those products that makes them interesting.

Keeping the enthusiasts (or the 90 per cent) engaged is a more basic proposition. Keeping them interested in what your brand has to say with creative posts and graphics creates a cohesive social media feed and encourages enthusiasts to lurk around for a longer period of time. I found this model extremely helpful to better understand the market of social media. Without understanding this model, one might waste time, money and energy. Imagine trying to understand the minds of all the enthusiasts out there who are just not interested in sharing your story—or ignoring someone who might have a huge, but not necessarily visible, following that can make your brand more successful.

If you need to conquer social media, the 1-9-90 model and its focus on the advocates is the way to go.

* * *

What makes a good product is more than just functionality but also user experience. By putting more emphasis and consideration on user experience, organizations in general, not just tech firms, can build better products for society. This is the promise of design thinking. Many experienced people have a healthy tendency to dismiss new buzzwords. We have grown used to industries routinely adopting new nomenclature every once in a while in order to breathe life into old concepts, and our spam filter gets set on the highest setting at this time every quarter.

A refreshing exception is the concept of 'design thinking', especially when used in relation to the enterprise software industry. While some industries have flirted with design thinking over the years, it has never really been mainstream except in a few. Design has been considered a creative endeavour, and not a commercial one, except, of course, if you are a design firm like Ideo or an Internet portal for designers like Dexigner.

Generation Y is beginning to change this dated viewpoint. There is a groundswell movement at management schools worldwide that focuses on the concept of design thinking, which starts with putting the user first.

For decades now, the development of software meant for business enterprises—whether for a new product or new versions of an old product—has followed methodologies where functionality (i.e., the process the software performs for a business) was paramount and the user was an afterthought. Many new methods of software development have been introduced over the years, such as waterfall development, use case development and now the latest—agile development. All these models are also used by myriad Internet start-ups. Most Internet start-ups are built with a particular business need in mind, such as retail (Amazon, Flipkart) and transportation (Uber, Ola). The user's ergonomic experience of the software has always been left to 'chemistry' which is a science different from computer programming. At best, the product has been updated for user-friendliness after it has been launched.

I will not bore you with a laboured explanation of each of these methods of software development, but will dally long enough to point out that whatever the method of development, 'user acceptance testing' was always the last and most hurried stage in the development of a new product meant for a business enterprise. This stage came much after the programming accuracy and the capability of the software to perform the business function were tested, and its robustness and integrity in an always-on 'production' environment was established through an intricate process known as 'regression testing'. The process—such as logistics, supply chain, accounting, mortgage processing and so on—that the system was capable of automating was paramount and the user's experience of using the system was secondary.

The concept of design thinking turns this process inside out. It begins with focusing on what users will want to experience, rather than on the commercial need the software will fulfil. This is a massive change, because it suddenly puts the thinking around ergonomics and beauty at the forefront—rather like Ferrari asking the famed automotive design house of Pininfarina to first design how its 'bella macchinas' would look and feel, before working on the motor and drivetrain.

Even in the automotive world, where one would expect to see it more often, such extreme design thinking is rare. New models are usually conjured up by automotive engineers who keep at the forefront considerations like engine performance, fuel efficiency and manufacturing automation through robots. They then throw this new product over the wall to a design studio that attempts to put a skin on the automobile to make it appealing to buyers.

In a stunning piece of forward thinking, India's house of Mahindra bought out the storied Pininfarina family business late in 2015. Assuming it's as affordable as the rest of Mahindra's stable, many would be more than willing to put down a security deposit on a Pininfarina-designed Mahindra car. Whether this acquisition benefits all parts of Mahindra—and especially its IT arm—is yet to be tested.

India's second-largest employer set, Indian software exporters, is now beginning to talk about design thinking as it relates to software in an attempt to get away from the 'factory' model of software services that they themselves quickly adopted in order to tease out more efficiency in the projects outsourced to them. In essence, it is an attempt to break free from the 'back office' tag that has been given to most Indian exporters of software services by attempting to occupy a space that promises to revolutionize software development the world over.

This shift is extreme, and is easier to talk about than accomplish.

* * *

Knowing the trajectory of tech development is paramount to understanding the possibilities of the future. The story of technological growth is rooted in the ability to analyse where technology has come from and explain the history of its development in order to point to its future. The first revolution in digital advertising occurred when Google began to place advertisements along with its standard web search results. Search Engine Optimization was all the rage a few years ago, which meant that companies were willing to spend money to ensure that a Google search for certain keywords would throw up their website within the first few hits. Simply put, these companies wanted to be on the first page of what Google served its users. The company was smart enough to add video to the mix, and now YouTube, with all its advertisements, operates as the second-largest search engine on the Internet.

The second revolution came along with Facebook, which with its own social media approach, created the largest advertising platform that the world had yet seen. Its purchase of WhatsApp, Instagram and other such players meant that it knew a lot about each one of us on its platforms, from who our associates were to what our areas of political, commercial, filial and artistic interests might be. And users, in droves, gave Facebook more information on their own likes and dislikes by putting up pictures of food, 'checking in' upon arriving at restaurants, theatres or other places of interest, and generally trying to best their online 'friends'. This gave the behemoth an untrammelled view of our personal lives, advertising grew significantly more finely targeted, and echo chambers came up that played information back to us that we were likely to approve of.

There is now a third revolution at hand. The world of broadcast television is going away, as our viewing screens become more and more Internet-connected for regular programming as well as for premium video feeds from channels such as Netflix, Amazon Video, Apple TV, YouTube TV and others. This is already apparent, at least in countries like the US (and soon in India as well, one can safely predict, with the current boom in Internet connectivity across the nation).

Programmatic advertising placement—targeted ads that are automatically placed online to appear on various Net-connected devices, including TV sets—is the third wave. This entails automating the buying and selling of advertisement slot inventory in real time through an automated bidding system. It enables advertisers or ad agencies to purchase advertisement impressions on publisher sites or apps within milliseconds through a sophisticated technological ecosystem. So far, this has been used mainly on mobile phones.

In the US, there are a few companies that are leading the way on programmatic advertising via connected TVs. The largest of these is The Trade Desk. The $26 billion California-based company, founded by chief executive officer Jeff Green, is a demand-side advertising platform that lets advertising agencies and other buyers place digital advertisements using algorithms and highly enriched data. This segment is growing far faster than the overall advertising market, but for now, it is still just a fraction of the latter's size.

The Trade Desk operates a cloud-based technology platform that lets advertisers optimize their ad spending, typically by getting the right advertisements to pop up for the right shoppers at the right time. Its stock had jumped almost 220 per cent right through the pandemic (though it has fallen a bit since). Early in November 2020, the company announced a huge positive surprise in its revenue and earnings for the preceding quarter.

As companies seek to rebuild their businesses after the pandemic, the typical measurement techniques that have been used by marketers are going to come under microscopic scrutiny by chief financial officers. And that means that advertisers have to focus on advertising opportunities that are measurable to the extent that returns generated for their business can be tracked and proven.

* * *

Though technology can change the structure of organizations and industries, we cannot use it as an excuse to cut corners in the pursuit of profit. Especially when it comes to exploiting workers. In 2019, California's legislature passed a watershed bill requiring companies like Uber, Lyft and Instacart to start treating their contract workers as employees. This is on the heels of a long-running debate on the topic. The bill, called Assembly Bill 5 (or simply AB5) became law on 1 January 2020 and ensured that workers are designated as employees if a company exerts control over how they perform their tasks as part of a company's regular business.

I called this a watershed bill since it is likely that the bill may influence other states. Labour groups have been advocating similar legislation in New York. In 2018, New York passed a minimum wage for ride-hailing drivers. At that time, however, it did not try to classify them as employees. Similar bills have been on the table in the states of Oregon and Washington but failed to advance. These could see renewed momentum. Across the pond, European countries have been grappling with the same issue. In India, ride-hailing firms and those with similar business models such as restaurant food delivery classify their workers as 'independent' businesspeople.

'Today, the so-called gig companies present themselves as the innovative future of tomorrow, a future where companies don't pay Social Security or Medicare,' according to California state senator Maria Elena Durazo. 'Let's be clear: there is nothing innovative about underpaying someone for their labour.' Until now, if workers thought they had been misclassified as contractors, it was up to them to fight the classification in court. But the bill allows Californian city governments to sue companies that don't comply. Dennis Herrera, San Francisco's city attorney, has signalled that he may act.

To my mind, this is good news for many gig economy workers who are bossed around and bullied by algorithms. As Joseph Campbell, an American author and professor who worked on comparative religion, put it many years ago, 'Computers are like Old Testament gods; lots of rules and no mercy.'

An example of Campbell's quote ringing true was brought home by an article in Bloomberg about Instacart, an app that 'outsources' grocery shopping and delivery. When Instacart's app gets a new order, it alerts a nearby worker who gathers and delivers the groceries. The app sends the order to the worker's phone with a bright green 'ACCEPT' button and a repetitive ping sound. But even if that worker—who supposedly has the flexibility to reject the task—decides the task isn't worth his or her time and effort, the app usually doesn't offer an option to decline. According to Bloomberg, workers are forced to mute their phone, close the app, or sit through some four minutes of loud pings. Those who wait it out sometimes wind up having to repeat the ordeal when the same task pops back up.

The costs imposed by the new bill could be very large for app-based businesses, many of which are not profitable. Uber held a troubled IPO in May 2019 and has reported large losses and slowing revenue growth. On a related note, at least until the pandemic began, public markets seemed much less friendly than venture capital and private equity funding rounds when it came to IPO valuations. Take WeWork's case. By the end of 2019, it looked like it would have to go public at 25 per cent of its last private valuation; this would have been a punishing 'down round' for SoftBank, which last invested over $10 billion in the 'flexi-office space' start-up at a valuation of over $40 billion.

Uber has laid off hundreds of employees (not drivers) in recent months to cut costs. Uber and other companies like it will likely mount a legal challenge to the bill and continue to claim that their drivers are not employees because they do not work in organized shifts. Tony West, chief legal officer of Uber, released a statement saying the bill doesn't apply to his ride-hailing company because driving for Uber takes place 'outside the usual course of Uber's business'. According to him, several previous rulings have found as much. He says Uber's business 'is serving as a technology platform for several different types of digital marketplaces'. He also said that the company was 'no stranger to legal battles'.

Some traditional firms, such as those in construction whose businesses were being 'disrupted' by market aggregators of the gig economy, will no doubt breathe more easily since their own models, which include paying for disability insurance coverage and other benefits for employees, will be less assailable. However, the problem with the California bill is that it could unintentionally affect many more Californians than just the gig economy workers who are bossed around and bullied by algorithms. Reports say that up to 1 million workers could be affected—not just those whom the bill is trying to protect, but many workers in relatively traditional businesses. For example, the *Wall Street Journal* reports that small vineyard owners in California who rely on contract labour for trucking out their harvests, religious groups that hire heads of their congregations as part-time contractors and franchisers with small businesses in the state will all be affected.

While legal challenges to such legislation are sure to ensue, I am glad that legislators are beginning to take note of such issues.

They might be a little more empathetic to their human brethren than die-hard capitalists or Old Testament gods.

* * *

Sometimes, even legislation is no match for capitalism. At times, capitalism can leave no room for empathy. During a US presidential election, other referendum choices are also on the ballot in each state. Take California's 2020 Proposition 22. It was critically important to firms such as Uber and Lyft. These gig economy businesses that use 'casual' workers had threatened to leave the state had the measure not been voted in. It wanted its drivers classified as contractors and not employees.

California is a left-leaning state and voted overwhelmingly for Joe Biden. Yet, Proposition 22 made it to the ballot. *Mint* reported in 2020 that gig economy ride-hailing apps spent over $200 million to see Proposition 22 through. Labour unions opposed to it could only muster about a tenth of that sum. The bigger money paid off. Over 58 per cent of California's voters opted to continue classifying drivers at these services as contractors.

Employee classification would have given rise to a slew of labour rights that today's gig workers, as 'independent contractors', do not enjoy. Workers for these gig companies in California will not have the same right as other employees to paid sick days, overtime pay, unemployment insurance or a workplace covered by occupational safety and health laws. California's Assembly had tried to head this off earlier with AB5, which would have guaranteed these rights. According to the LA Times, one lawmaker, who wrote AB5 and opposed Proposition 22, said: 'Instead of paying their drivers, gig corporations forged a deceptive $204-million campaign to change the rules for themselves and provide their workers with less than our state laws require.'

California's voters seem to have a curious inclination to set right-wing precedents by adopting state-level propositions at the ballot. Smart or misleading campaigns run before elections tend to sway voters' opinions in this otherwise left-leaning state. In 2020, gig companies put out a message that they would pay their contractors more than the minimum wage. This appears to have caught voters' attention and led them on. They were bombarded with emails, glossy fliers, text messages and video spots. The truth, however, according to the National Employment Law Project (NELP), was that someone driving an average of 35km every hour in a 40-hour workweek would make $287 less per week if Proposition 22 passed. This is in addition to a slew of healthcare and other reductions. The NELP says a 'permanent underclass of workers' has been created.

Before 2020's Proposition 22, a 1994 proposal in California removed the right of 'illegal aliens' to seek recourse to public funds. This meant that even if non-US-citizens had been paying income taxes or real estate levies for the properties that they lived in, they (and their children) would be ineligible for public benefits such as basic schooling, which is largely free in the US, as well as healthcare and other social benefits. It's hard to imagine why an electorate that is left-leaning would deny taxpayers their rights. But then, election marketing has proven itself effective.

The day after the 1994 proposition was approved by the state's voters, several groups filed federal lawsuits against it. A US federal district court judge issued a temporary injunction against the state of California, forbidding the enforcement of that proposition. Another federal judge issued a permanent injunction, pending a trial. The state of California asked in 1997 that the trial be dismissed and the injunction dropped, on the grounds that US immigration law had changed in the meantime. The federal court left the permanent injunction standing.

Coming back to Proposition 22, equity markets have reacted positively. For instance, despite suffering losses, Uber's stock has managed to emerge largely unscathed. Uber's loss before interest and tax had deepened to $625 million in 2020's third quarter. Its sales declined 18 per cent to $3.1 billion, even as the pandemic continues to dampen travel spend. Its business prospects would certainly have been much worse if Uber hadn't won a reprieve from California's electorate.

Gig businesses will take heart from the victory in California and hope to replicate this success across the US (and I daresay beyond its shores). Emboldened by the result in California, Uber and the others will move similar legislation in other US states. These could include New Jersey and Massachusetts, where state regulators have made them uncomfortable, or New York or Pennsylvania, where courts have rejected their argument that workers run their own independent businesses as contractors.

In India, we are somewhat isolated from such issues. Our disposition towards 'informal economy' workers has had laissez-faire attitudes. This is largely because India has long had a mobile lower-class population that often migrates from one state to another in search of work and a livelihood. We tend to look askance at this population, falling as they do among India's teeming poor. It's thus a surprise to see an attempt at ensuring that food delivery boys and ride-hailing drivers get some social security benefits under a revised labour code. Whether gig employers will resist this remains unknown.

What next? Will there be a replay of 1994's events with Proposition 22 being challenged in a national court? Civil rights and labour unions have vowed to initiate cases. Or will big tech's money and marketing pizzazz win the day? We will have to deal with these issues in India as well, and the government is responding with laws meant to regulate the role of big tech. Even so, it is likely that big tech will try to influence opinion. I am torn either way. On one hand, light regulation is good for business. On the other, it leaves room for exploitation.

* * *

New frontiers of technology mean new methods of political fighting and power can emerge. With new rules, there's a lot more to consider on the future of society and nations in general. None more so than China versus the US.

Many years ago, while I was on a phone call with a colleague in the US, he loudly proclaimed mid-call that he was a patriot who had served his country's military 'just to be clear for the Great Recorder of all phone calls'. Needless to say, I was intrigued by his behaviour. My interlocutor had been mildly critical of the US's then immigration policy for skilled technical workers, but had said nothing out of the ordinary, and nothing which had not already been reported to the press. When I pressed him on why he had interrupted the conversation with his proclamation, he replied that he suspected that the US government had access to all phone calls made from or to the US.

This call occurred long before 2013, when Edward Snowden disclosed that the National Security Agency (NSA) had indeed been accessing calls for a long time. A quiet executive order passed by then President George W. Bush in the wake of the 9/11 attacks had given broad, sweeping powers to the NSA, and it was indeed monitoring call data records (CDRs). As actions like these require ratification, a secret court hearing allowed Bush's order to be implemented. Given that the US was reeling after what was essentially an act of war, it is not surprising that the court ratification happened without much public discourse. Most Americans were blissfully unaware that their government was indeed spying on them. Snowden had his US passport revoked for making that disclosure and spent over a month in the transit lounge at Moscow's international airport before finally being given asylum by that country.

Expectedly, Snowden's disclosure raised privacy concerns in the US. The US Congress replaced Bush's programme with the USA Freedom Act in 2015. The Act expired at the end of 2019, but it appears that the NSA is no longer interested in obtaining billions of CDRs every day. In a *New York Times* article in 2019, that paper asserts that the NSA's programme had not been used in months and that the NSA had quietly shut it down.

This is not a surprise. On 28 June 2018, the NSA itself issued a press announcement saying it was deleting CDRs. An excerpt from that announcement states, 'Because it was infeasible to identify and isolate properly produced data, NSA concluded that it should not use any of the CDRs.' This could well be because the NSA realizes that it has other tools at its command, including access to detailed location data for the billions of people worldwide who use big tech platforms. Today's big tech companies are all US-based and that is where their data resides. Despite Apple Inc.'s capitulation in 2018 to the Chinese government, where it promised to keep data from Chinese iCloud users in China, other firms have exited the Chinese market. Besides, being a US company, it is entirely possible that Apple keeps a mirror of its China users' data in a database that resides in the US. The fact that this data is available to US intelligence agencies on their own native soil allows them the comfort that they can always access such data should they want or need to.

In a separate area, there is now news that the NSA has released a powerful open-source reverse-engineering hacking tool called Ghidra into the public domain. Ghidra reduces programming code down to the level of 'assembler' language, which is an expression of programming code down to the level of machine-level instructions into the binary 1s and 0s that are understood by computer chips. Tools like these exist today but cost a large amount of money to procure. Ghidra's release levels the playing field and has been welcomed by many. However, not all experts are convinced that this is a selfless gesture, because they believe that the Ghidra code may well have 'back doors' into computer systems and telecommunications networks.

Meanwhile, the NSA and its sister agencies are making sure that non-US governments will not have an easy time if they seek to access similar back doors to user data. In February 2018, six top US intelligence chiefs from the NSA, CIA, FBI and other agencies told a US Senate committee that they believed that China's Huawei and ZTE were not to be trusted because they could allow China's government a back door into communications infrastructure, thereby giving Chinese intelligence agencies broad access to personal data and other sensitive information. The FBI director at the time, Chris Ray, testified, 'We're deeply concerned about the risks of allowing any company or entity that is beholden to foreign governments that don't share our values to gain positions of power inside our telecommunications networks.'

Huawei now faces a ban on its equipment in the US as legislation passed in 2018 restricted its equipment in the US. The company is now suing the US government, calling the move 'unconstitutional'. Huawei's chief financial officer Meng Wanzhou, the daughter of founder Ren Zhengfei, faces potential extradition from Canada to the US over charges of Iran sanction violations. Despite the ban and Meng's detention, Huawei is now a force to contend with. Its 2018 revenue was $109 billion, just a smidgen short of Microsoft Inc.'s $110 billion. It is also now one of the world's largest smartphone makers, having eclipsed Apple some time ago.

It appears that the background battle between American and Chinese intelligence agencies for hegemony over sensitive data is yet another frontier in the ongoing US–China trade war.

* * *

The debate about the sustainability impacts caused by heavy industry and by the extractors of oil and resources is well known. The flashpoints against these firms are usually mounted by local activists and are rarely experienced at a national, let alone, global level. Nonetheless, such local action can be extremely potent.

Less obvious, and therefore insidious, is the effect that technology firms can have on the environment. IT is not an environmentally clean industry. This topic is too large to cover in one small musing, but I will attempt to open up a discussion here. Beyond the socio-cultural or even economic value of technology, one must also look at the effect that technology growth has on other areas of life, such as the environment—I've written earlier about the amount of energy being consumed by new technologies, and the fact that some of these also use more electricity than many countries do. Closer to home, the IT boom has laid waste to Indian cities that are seen as technology hubs.

Much more worrisome than annoying traffic jams and pollution caused by office-going IT programmers in India is the overall pivot that the world's IT industry is making towards pervasive AI. Today's AI boom is actually, in large part, simply a renaissance of AI concepts that are decades old. These old concepts have now turned into reality because they finally have a huge step up in computing and data crunching power, which happens to be extremely energy-hungry.

Companies such as Google and Facebook run massive data centres and consume immense amounts of energy. This computing power is needed to crunch through data and provide immediate results for decades-old algorithms so that they can be delivered to your smartphone in a flash—and entice you to linger or buy the products being advertised.

And now, new strictures around data privacy and accuracy have created even more demand for energy. Search engines such as Google scrape in data from various sources and use AI-centric data crunching to provide results. Search results can be gamed, however, and there is an entire sub-industry around Search Engine Optimization, which seeks to trick search algorithms into giving its clients more prominence.

Vandals who actively falsify such data abound. Google recently listed Nazism as the ideology of the California Republican Party. This is false, of course, but it evidently came from Wikipedia, which is known for crowdsourced data, and has lax policing. A vandal had been able to add Nazism as an influence on to the Republican Party's Wikipedia page. Google's search engines picked up the 'N' word but weren't able to filter it out.

Meanwhile, Facebook's problems with data privacy, false news and hate speech are well documented. In response, tech companies have been spending even more on 'listening' AI algorithms, using training data to spot patterns and nip false news in the bud. This means more computing power will be needed. Facebook indicated that its total expenses would grow from 45 per cent to 60 per cent, partly due to spending on AI monitoring of questionable content.

The electricity we use does not generate itself. Much of it comes from burning fossil fuels such as coal, and environmental pollution is a result. Renewable energy sources are still not pervasive enough to replace fossil fuel use. Whether former US President Donald Trump or I want to believe it or not, science has overwhelmingly established that humans are contributing to global warming by burning fossil fuels.

In a fascinating turn of events, it seems local environmental activists now have the ability to use global concerns for local action. A few years ago, seven Californian cities started a lawsuit against local oil companies for contributing to global warming that has substantially eroded their coastlines. The oil companies contend they can't be held responsible simply for extracting the resource and that the real threat comes from resource users, big tech included.

How the local courts handle this will be interesting and may well set a precedent. After all, it wasn't tobacco growers who were sued for lung cancer deaths—it was the cigarette manufacturers.

* * *

It is not a universal truth that technology can solve every problem for society. Consider the situation of mental health treatment. The COVID-19 pandemic has changed the prism of tech investing in such a way that it now seems to reveal many more colours than it normally would—i.e., the seven colours of a rainbow that form the basic spectrum of white light. The investing world, both in public as well as private markets, now seems to believe that the application of technology to a problem can somehow deliver a solution that appeared impossible to find just a few months earlier.

This is especially true of start-ups in the telemedicine arena. Medical payers, providers and equipment manufacturers had long attempted to use telemedicine in an attempt to increase profits and provide care to patients in far-flung areas without easy access to doctors. Despite the existence of the Internet, online platforms for video conferencing, and sophisticated peripheral 'smart' devices in patients' homes (or on their wrists), telemedicine never really came into its own before the pandemic. This is because physical interaction between doctors and patients is an integral part of the healing process. Medical procedures like vaccinations and surgeries need to be performed on patients, of course, but even when it comes to regular consultation, healing is a holistic process. It cannot be robotized.

Some years ago, John Fox, a former professor at Oxford and an expert at the intersection of AI and medicine, said to me that psychologists have known for a long time that human decision-making is flawed, even if sometimes amazingly creative, and overconfidence is an important source of error in routine settings. A large part of the motivation for applying AI to medicine comes from the knowledge that to err is human and that overconfidence is an established cause of clinical mistakes. Overconfidence is a human failing, and not that of a machine; it has a huge influence on our personal and collective successes and failures.

That, however, was an earlier view. We now know that bias can and does creep into AI programs, too. Earlier in this book, I have discussed Generative Pre-trained Transformer 3 (GPT-3), a new deep-learning technology that holds promise as a programming assistant. It is based on billions of words picked up as part of its 'learning' curriculum on the Internet. Its creators have been very careful about when and how much of it they will release for general use. While the commercial incentive to create a 'cheat sheet' computer programming language for everyone must certainly be large, its creators have been reticent, as they have recognized that a lot of what is said on the Internet (especially on social media) is hateful, racist and biased, and so the widespread use of GPT-3 before it is purged of such biases would yield net negative outcomes.

* * *

The development and growth of technology can drastically change the nature of life in society. Such drastic changes in lifestyle require immense adaptability and moving forward requires an understanding that not everybody can adapt. We need to be able to and be willing to provide a helping hand to those who struggle with these changes. Many businesses spend time trying to understand the millennial generation and especially their interaction with technology. As a father of two children who can be classified among this generation, or at least in the generation that succeeded it—Generation Y—this topic is of personal interest to me. I have written before of how forward-thinking organizations, such as Commonsense.org, attempt to explain these new generations and their online behaviours. My sister, a Harvard PhD in psychology, used to work for this organization and has shared many tips with me on how to react to, and sometimes regulate, my children's online behaviour. They are now adults, but I still often wonder whether I did the right things by them.

Almost all the research being done on these generations and their interaction with technology is based out of the West, where the penetration of technology and the Internet has been high. India, however, is another situation altogether. That said, it is true that, like most parents worldwide of millennials and Generation Y, we were introduced to technology and immediate access to the Internet at the same time as our children were. We were as lost as any parent in the US or UK in shepherding our children's use of technology.

But India has its own characteristics that affected Generation X, viz. my generation, very differently than our contemporaries in the Western world. We grew up during India's licence raj and our access to technology—even television—was limited. Our childhood was not much different from our parents'; our extracurricular activities were the same gully cricket and hopscotch. I grew up without TV, which wasn't introduced in Bengaluru until I had finished school. And even then, all we had was a few hours of programming, on one channel. My father believed that TV was an 'idiot box' and did not procure a TV for the home until I had left the country for postgraduate studies. Judging by the squawking on Indian TV today, he was right.

So, the neat definitions of Generation X, millennials and Generation Y that researchers in the US make are less applicable to Indians. We are finding new patterns in Indian behaviour online that don't bear any resemblance to patterns observed in the West. The Western press has found it entertaining enough to pen condescending articles on how Indians are 'choking' the Internet by sending each other 'good morning' messages. Meanwhile, an entire set of start-ups as well as established firms are trying to find ways to appeal to the waking giant represented by 'Bharat'—the newly online Indians who don't speak English.

Many investors back the Bharat phenomenon mindlessly by betting that its 'network' effects will explode. The last time firms took a similar bet, with basic wireless and cellular technology, all they had in return was the 'missed call' effect. Smart Indian users figured out that they could call someone and then quickly hang up, secure in the knowledge that the recipient knew they were trying to reach them. Smart firms used this uniquely Indian behaviour to interact with potential customers. This frugal behaviour caused mobile operators' revenue projections to plummet. We now have one of the lowest revenues per user wireless markets in the world.

Nonetheless, there are many opportunities in the workplace for connecting Indian millennials and Generation Y to not just the older ones among us but also to the waking giant of Bharat. But with Bharat, the gap is more like how our parents would relate to technology when introduced to it by their grandchildren. Even in the

US, which dubs this generation 'the silent generation', the uptake in online use is quite low; only 30 per cent of them use smartphones, according to the Pew Research Center.

So how can our youth help? First off, by helping to evangelize the use of technology. Previous generations often seek help from millennials for training on untapped shortcuts and features, on both personal as well as commercial applications. Training first-time users in Bharat on such processes will come easier for the younger generations who were born with a smartphone in their hands.

The reverse is also true. Preceding generations can teach millennials personal behaviour characteristics which have been jeopardized by technology. The one personal characteristic I keep harping on with youngsters is developing the ability to focus all of one's attention on a single task. Clichés like 'Women can multitask, unlike men' and 'Youngsters can look at a half-dozen screens at the same time' are bogus. My experience is that humans can only be productive when they focus on a single task at a time. Developing such focus comes with learning how to still the mind.

Several charlatans peddle their wares in this department by calling it spiritual 'enlightenment', which it is not. One can learn to concentrate through several methods—of which the practice of meditation is just one. Man has forever looked to find ways to still his own mind. Learning music and exercise forms such as yoga, martial arts and complex dance forms work just as well as meditation in order to develop our 'concentration' muscles. Yet, the continued practice of meditation and prayer, which many of our elders and those in Bharat developed, can be used to learn to take life as it comes and on its own terms. Then there is the art of managing interpersonal interactions that they had to develop to thrive in an era of scarcity, which the younger generations will benefit from.

The easy relationship between millennials and Generation Y with technology is here to stay. Despite the negative connotations associated with technology and these generations, technology can harness new positives for both young and old. And, importantly, for 'Bharat'—as some industry players call the vast hinterland of India that is now coming online.

* * *

Advances in technology do not necessarily benefit everybody in the world. Understanding this concept is important for figuring out a path towards a future where technology benefits all of human society and not just the privileged. It may be time for a supranational body similar to the World Health Organization to be constituted to help govern the world of technology. My argument is that, to some degree at least, technology is a public good, just as basic health is, and its benefits need to be shared across a larger swathe of the world's population.

In a scathing article in the *Financial Times*, Chandran Nair, founder of the Global Institute for Tomorrow, argues that the technology giants of today, such as Microsoft, completely ignore the fact that the majority of the world's population—especially those in developing countries—are still stuck in a pre-industrial age, and that technology as the developed world knows it—search engines, e-commerce, artificial intelligence, virtual reality and so on—are of no use to people who have to still practise pre-industrial techniques such as slash-and-burn farming in order to survive.

He talks of the yearly haze that blankets countries such as Singapore and Malaysia, when farmers in Indonesia burn their oil palm crop every year so that they can plant anew (a phenomenon we are well aware of in north India and Delhi/NCR as well)—while developers and IT executives sit in air-conditioned rooms and hold conferences about the future of technology, blissfully unaware of pre-industrial age social problems, such as where to find a toilet. He claims that when a question about this deep digital divide was posed to Microsoft, the spokesperson's answer was: 'This is a question for a futurist to ponder, and not one for technologists to worry about.'

The lopsided distribution of technology benefits is a known fact, but regulators are flummoxed with how to deal with the problem. Regulation—or governmental activism—to date has been focused only on three vectors. First, the attempt to break monopolistic market power held by a few corporations. Second, an attempt to mop up a larger share of the tax pie when such companies experience enormous profits. And third, a clumsy attempt to protect privacy by forcing data on customers to stay in the country where it was first generated.

At the beginning of this century, Microsoft was hit by US regulators who found that its Internet Explorer, which was bundled with Windows software, was an attempt to shut out other Internet browsers, and forced to pay a hefty fine for indulging in monopolistic practices. The European Union (EU) is now trying to force search engines to not use their market power to coerce content providers such as news organizations to provide their information for free on their search engine sites. YouTube has been banned in China, and Google simply shut down operations in Spain when the Spaniards tried to charge a levy on Google aggregating content from news organizations and then providing this news for free for users of its search engine or mobile operating systems.

Tax legislation, sometimes even grandfathered to defeat judgements handed down by an apex court—as happened in the famed Vodafone India tax case—is an example of a national government going to great lengths to use policy to widen its tax net, or the second vector.

We now have WhatsApp using a change in its privacy policy to hand over its users' information to Facebook, its parent, after first claiming that no one, not even WhatsApp, can see the content of the messages that its users send to one another. WhatsApp, of course, claims that this data is only going to be used for it to 'explore ways in which its users can interact with businesses that matter to them without being subjected to third-party banner ads and spam'. Well, okay, but Daddy Facebook is even rumoured to have algorithms that can predict when two of its users are falling in love with one another.

Most outsourcers in India are hampered by EU privacy laws, which mandate that personal data regarding European citizens needs to stay in Europe. Streamlined, supranational legislation in this area—governing the capture and use of personal data, and the nature of the myriad personal relationships that individuals have with one another online—will be necessary soon. The present clumsy laws need to change.

Regulation has not yet addressed the fourth vector—the use of technology for the common good. In one of my recent discussions with Kashyap Kompella, the CEO of rp2ai, he spoke of the need for an 'Indian Technology Service' to be included among India's civil service agencies. This, he argued, could support the formation of unified policies for bringing technological benefits to the poor, as well as making sure that data privacy issues are managed with no negative impact on the citizenry.

My take is that while such national, governmental bodies are necessary so that each country can form its own technology policies, there are certain aspects of the rapid advance of technology that can only be governed and managed through supranational bodies that ensure a modicum of egalitarian distribution of the positive aspects of technology (i.e., technology's characteristics as a public good) and the negative aspects (data piracy, identity theft and other such public dangers posed by cyber criminals) are policed and kept to a minimum. In all seriousness, I would vote that China be the first president of this body. It is the one country that has been able to crack down on big tech—both home-grown and international. While 'big government' is a concern among democratic nations, big tech is, to my mind, a much larger concern. In a democracy, where governments tended to be voted in and out, I would rather hand some of my freedoms over to the government rather than to a faceless corporation.

* * *

Technology, by its nature, is meant to be dispassionate. Decisions are made by reason and not emotion. But the application of technology to industries such as weapons manufacturing means that before AI can reach the point where it can make decisions for itself, humans will be the ones to 'pull the trigger'. We must understand the effect of this process on the individuals involved. The redefinition of jobs as we know them is what troubles us most about recent advances in AI. AI-based novels may be here by 2030, and AI surgery by 2050, depending on whom you believe. We fear 'singularity', the point at which AI crosses over and is independently capable of re-engineering and reinventing itself without human assistance—and is smarter than what any human trying to control it could be.

Jobs, or singularity, are far from what should be worrying us the most about the advances in AI. To my mind, the AI-based development of autonomous weaponry, which to some extent is already happening, is far more frightening. Autonomous weapons can decide for themselves when to take human lives.

Automated weaponry is not new. In 1884, Hiram Maxim invented the first machine gun, and in the last century, man's foray into the skies was soon followed by sky-based warfare. After a while, sky-based warfare became more automated—from intercontinental ballistic missiles that are launched and controlled from afar, and can cause widespread destruction, to the pinpoint accuracy of killer military drones that are piloted from thousands of miles away and can be aimed to kill just a single man. But these weapons are not autonomous, since they all still have a human being at the trigger end. It is that human who must take the final decision to snuff out one—or many—lives.

Despite patriotism and the drilled-in willingness to follow orders, human beings who decide when to pull a trigger or drop a bomb can pay a high psychological price. Remorse and post-traumatic stress disorder (PTSD) often dog those who have been in combat situations. Charles Sweeney, who dropped the second atom bomb on Nagasaki, said before he died: 'As the man who commanded the last atomic mission, I pray that I retain that singular distinction.' This is quite obviously not so of a machine that makes such a decision, and by extension, the scientists and researchers who build them. I doubt Hiram Maxim faced PTSD, though many who actually pulled the trigger on his machine guns most certainly did.

China has now begun to recruit and train youngsters for its autonomous weapons programme. On 8 November 2018, the *South China Morning Post* reported that Beijing Institute of Technology (BIT) had announced on its website that it had selected thirty-one students, all under the age of eighteen, to begin training as the world's youngest AI weapons scientists. More than 5000 high school students had applied for the programme. The thirty-one were not selected solely for their intellectual aptitude; they were also screened for other qualities such as creative thinking, a willingness to fight, persistence when facing challenges, 'passion' for developing new weapons and patriotism, according to a BIT professor. Other countries will follow suit.

These are not just autonomous conventional weapons but could also be microscopic robots that can crawl into human blood vessels. When used in weaponry, AI will be a horror long before it achieves singularity.

* * *

The great changes to industries that technology promises and follows through on will cause upheaval. Those workers who are displaced by rising tech will not only be unhappy but will also fight back against the implementation of new tech. This is another big effect of tech advances that we must pay attention to. It is becoming extremely clear that executives from big tech companies are coming under increasing fire from at least three different groups in addition to governments.

The first is with the stock markets. Like Google, governmental discomfiture with Facebook has been on show publicly. To add to this, more recent news is out that Facebook has had yet another breach where users' photographs have been shared without their knowledge. Across town, Apple Inc. has stopped disclosing unit sales for its iPhone products. In the meantime, its suppliers have forecast weakening demand for their components that are used in Apple's iPhones—thereby creating jitters among investors, and a steep fall in Apple's stock price. On 14 December 2018, Apple was trading at $165, down from $232 on 3 October.

Big tech firms' troubles don't stop with lawmakers and stock market investors. They are now coming under fire from human rights groups who are united in their viewpoint, and are working together to limit the activities of big tech. Bloomberg reported in 2018 that more than sixty human rights groups, including Amnesty International and Human Rights Watch, demanded Google end an effort to launch a censored search engine in China, saying the move could make the company 'complicit in human rights violations'.

Early in 2018, the company was besieged by organizations that normally reserve their ire for weapons manufacturers. These organizations were protesting an AI contract that Google had signed with the US's Pentagon (or defence establishment) and were asking for its cancellation.

In May 2018, the International Committee for Robot Arms Control wrote in an open letter to Google employees: 'We are deeply concerned about the possible integration of Google's data on people's everyday lives with military surveillance data, and its combined application to targeted killing . . . Google has moved into military work without subjecting itself to public debate or deliberation, either domestically or internationally.'

But most interesting of all is the discontent among employees that is fomenting within these firms. Employee activism is on the rise. Google decided in 2018 that it would let the Pentagon contract lapse after employees threatened to quit over the matter. Such employee activism has also been seen at other firms. The *Atlantic* reports that Microsoft employees have protested their company's contract with the US Immigration and Customs Enforcement in an open letter, saying that the company should put 'children and families over profits'. In addition, Amazon's employees have asked Jeff Bezos, their boss and one of the world's richest men, to cease selling face-recognition software to law enforcement for fear that it may be misused.

This collective conscience of white-collar tech employees is vastly different from blue-collar unionization. Unions typically deal with workplace issues such as compensation and safe working conditions, and not with the societal issues that have caught the imagination of big tech's employees.

Epilogue

With the world changing so rapidly, it can be difficult to keep up and it can feel overwhelming to even try. That is why it is of utmost importance to learn how to handle oneself in the face of great change.

About a decade ago, I was diagnosed with cancer. The lab results from that morning's tests came in just as I was on an evening call with colleagues in the US, trying to decide on a seemingly important but actually trivial corporate matter. The fear when I read the report was so visceral that I abruptly ended the call, without proffering a reason to my astonished co-workers. They found out why only much later.

Thanks to my doctors and thanks to a greater force I shall today call 'balance', and which others may call 'god' or 'nature', the cancer is behind me.

But balance didn't leave me unchanged. So, for now at least, I will leave it to the pundits to predict what might happen to information technology in the aftermath of these strange times. Also left to them are the tortuous financial arithmetic and recommendations on what industry or government should now do.

I am going to dwell instead on how the human mind can adapt to gut-wrenching turmoil. This is not yet another pop-psychology blurb on the five stages of loss; it is a personal account of the types of techniques we have to turn to when we find ourselves defenceless and alone, fighting a baffling, cunning and powerful enemy.

Just as in Chapter 12, I will again share three techniques that I attempted to use then, as I will no doubt have to yet again. I am nowhere near perfect in applying these. I claim no pride of authorship; I am only trying to write about a few eternal truths which could help us make sense of it all—if only we work to develop the capacity to reflect upon these truths.

The first is to accept that Nature's harmony (or god or spirit or whatever you call it) is greater than us. The second is to create space in our minds to better witness our own thoughts and, therefore, purposefully respond to difficult times instead of immediately reacting to circumstances. The third is to use our freedom of will; to respond with actions in consonance with the direction of Nature's harmony, and not against it.

Age-old wisdom lays down the law of cause and effect as a profound truth. This truth has been twisted down the ages by tech potentates, politicians, and in some cases even our parents, who attempt to manipulate our thinking and control our psyches. Addictive social networking apps are an example. The manipulators profit from the fact that our minds are unwilling to accept that our world ceaselessly changes and that our bubbles pop. Humankind clings to a need for control so strongly that we want to continue to influence this world from even beyond our graves, and so the toiling middle-class writes out wills and testaments while tech potentates make grandiose bequests to charity.

But the untwisted law of cause and effect lays down that everything that happens in the universe is in balance. Various great teachings have laid emphasis on this underlying point of balance. Every event that happens contributes to the balance of the whole; it is all one system, even though a single event within the system may seem utterly incomprehensible.

The harmony of this balance inspired Albert Einstein to say, 'The scientist's religious feeling takes the path of a rapturous amazement at the harmony of natural law, which reveals an intelligence of such superiority that, compared with it, all the systematic thinking and acting of human beings is an utterly insignificant reflection.'

When we create enough space to be witnesses to ourselves, we are free to choose our responses, and therefore alter the reality we experience. And only human beings can do that, not automatons or computers or robots. These are soulless beings, bereft of sentience, and as a result, can never be a witness to their own machinations. They can only react in the manner their set of computer instructions tells them to. They can never respond. We, as human beings, however, can choose to respond instead of reacting.

We best respond by developing some sort of personal peace pact with the harmony that is larger than us, as described by Einstein, and then by going about using our free will in accordance with that harmony; not in opposition to it. Maybe, as Alfred, Lord Tennyson wrote: 'More things are wrought by prayer than this world dreams of.' Or if you prefer a secular quote, here is Carl Jung: 'Who looks outside, dreams; who looks inside, awakes.'